RULE ON CRIME

ANDREW RULE

Published by:
Wilkinson Publishing Pty Ltd
ACN 006 042 173
Level 4, 2 Collins Street
Melbourne, Vic 3000
Ph: 03 9654 5446
www.wilkinsonpublishing.com.au

Copyright © 2024 Andrew Rule

All rights reserved. No part of this publication may be reproduced, stored in a retrieval system or transmitted in any form by any means without the prior permission of the copyright owner. Enquiries should be made to the publisher.

Every effort has been made to ensure that this book is free from error or omissions. However, the Publisher, the Author, the Editor or their respective employees or agents,
shall not accept responsibility for injury, loss or damage occasioned to any person acting or refraining from action as a result of material in this book whether or not such injury, loss or damage is in any way due to any negligent act or omission, breach of duty or default on the part of the Publisher, the Author, the Editor, or their respective employees or agents.

National Library of Australia Cataloguing-in-Publication entry

Creator: Rule, Andrew, 1957- author.

Title: Rule on crime / Andrew Rule.

ISBN: 9781923259089 (paperback)

Subjects: Crime
        Australia.Criminals
        Australia.Criminal investigation
        Australia.Cold cases (Criminal investigation)
        Australia.

Cover and Internal design by Spike Creative Pty Ltd
Ph: (03) 9427 9500
spikecreative.com.au

Reprint 2025

CONTENTS

Murder on Easey Street 5

The harder they fall 25

The Shootist.. 49

Girls who like bad boys.. 75

It's payback time 107

A sashimi deal 131

The one that got away.. 149

The suicide that wasn't 173

Falling down 215

The finger of suspicion 231

Still looking for the Beaumont children 243

CHAPTER 1
MURDER ON EASEY STREET

In The 1970s the young and restless skated from job to job, bed to bed, across the thin ice of a suddenly permissive age.

After four decades and too many false leads, the slow-motion quest to solve Australia's most notorious double murder finally led cold case investigators to do something that could and probably should have been done many years before.

They made a list with 131 names on it, knowing that 90 of those persons of interest were still alive and that the relatives of dead ones could be tested. The detectives' best guess was that one of those names would unlock the mystery of the Easey Street murders.

The killing of lifelong friends Suzanne Armstrong and Susan Bartlett had happened at the height of an Australian summer, in January, 1977, in a street whose name would echo down the years — Easey Street, Collingwood.

The long list of 2017 was long overdue but, in fact, it wasn't the first Easey Street list. A much shorter one of just eight potential suspects had been made shortly after the murders. The police back then were confident the killer was one of the eight. But when the forensic breakthrough of DNA testing became a reality in the 1990s, the potent new science showed those assumptions were wrong: no one on the shortlist was a match with the presumed killer's DNA sample taken from Suzanne Armstrong's body. That disappointing result was to sideline the investigation for another generation.

It was only when a review was ordered well into the new century that investigators pulled every possible name from the 1970s paperwork: names of men who had been interviewed, had been nominated or were the target of tip-offs after the murders. Many names might have been mentioned in the homicide file but others were most likely plucked from other contemporary police documents, such as the running sheets and log books of local police. At least one name cropped up in both those sources.

A few days after the murders, a young uniformed Collingwood policeman pulled over a local youth in a car for a routine check. The policeman was Ron Iddles, who would later go on to make his name as a homicide detective.

The youth in the car was one of the sons of a Greek migrant couple who then lived at 3 Bendigo Street, a few blocks from the murder house, 147 Easey Street.

One version of his name was Periklis Kouroumblis. He called himself 'Perry' and was known to police for relatively minor offences around the district. His family surname, relatively rare in Greece, was often spelled an alternative way, 'Kouroumplis', which is how it appeared on at least some of his Greek identification papers years later. Whether this tiny glitch was enough to obscure his movements or identity is hard to say.

The keen young constable checked the car that the teenager was in. In the boot he found a long-bladed knife in a leather sheath. It apparently had a slightly bent tip and some blood staining in the sheath. Iddles took the knife, making sure it was handed to the crime department at Russell Street police headquarters. Ten days after the murders, newspapers photographed the knife held by a detective chief inspector, Eric Janetzski, who appealed for any information about who might have bought or sold the weapon, which looked new and had never been re-sharpened.

The key question was how and when Perry Kouroumblis, alias Periklis Kouroumplis, had come by the knife. His story, which he told Iddles and repeated in a robust homicide interrogation, was that he'd found it on or near the tracks at Victoria Park rail station late on the night of the murders — Monday, 10 January.

The blade was clean but the blood stain in the scabbard was enough for forensics to establish that it was Group A, a relatively common blood group that happened to match Suzanne Armstrong's.

The police bought Perry Kouroumblis's story and then tried to find out who'd bought the knife. They canvassed hardware and army disposal stores in an attempt to trace its history but the lead fizzled out. And that's where the investigation stalled for 40 years.

Except, that is, for a minor flurry of activity a few years after Australian police widely adopted DNA testing in the 1990s. A decade after DNA was first used in a Canberra rape case, someone decided to apply it using the lost-and-found sample originally taken from Suzanne Armstrong's body nearly 22 years earlier.

It led to a scene straight from a gritty British police procedural. In December 1998, in the depths of an English winter, two Australian investigators shivered with cold as they waited to play the last card in a game they hoped would trap a killer with a macabre secret.

With the Australians were two Scotland Yard detectives, who'd narrowed the search to the building they were watching: a drab office in a drab street in Margate, a shabby holiday town on the Kent coast smelling of fish and chip fat and poverty.

They didn't know their quarry's exact address, but computer checks showed he had been collecting his dole money from this particular office. It was payday. He was sure to turn up.

Sure enough, the man collected his dole, and the detectives collected him. Detective Sergeant Steve Tragardh and his boss, Chief Inspector Rod Collins, had agreed to let Scotland Yard do the talking, so the nomadic suspect wouldn't be alarmed by knowing immediately why he might be wanted a world away.

They took him to the local police station, the Yard men saying all they needed was a tiny blood sample — a routine precaution, they said soothingly, which would eliminate him from a local inquiry.

The suspect gave it willingly, so willingly that Tragardh and Collins astutely wondered right then if it was a wild goose chase.

Tragardh pocketed the vial of blood, and they returned to London to extradite another murder suspect, which was the official reason for their flying visit. The detective kept the blood sample safely in his possession until he handed it over to the staff at the Victoria Police forensic science centre back in Melbourne.

Days later, a forensic expert compared the DNA code in the English blood sample with DNA from what was coyly called a 'body fluid' taken from the crime scene almost exactly 22 years before. The fluid was semen, and it had been found underneath the blood-stained body of Suzanne Armstrong and had been re-discovered in 1997 with other Easey Street exhibits mislaid in storage for years.

Suzanne, 27, had been stabbed more than 20 times, and police assumed she had been raped as she was dying, discounting any other possibility that might explain the presence of semen. Susan Bartlett had been stabbed more than 50 times, presumably after coming to her friend's aid.

When the forensic scientists compared the English sample with the now very old crime scene sample, it was negative. One by one the suspects had been eliminated. Now there were no more and the investigation was back exactly to where it was when the bodies were found on a shockingly hot day in 1977. After more than 20 years, the trail was colder than ever.

Suzanne Armstrong had turned 21 in 1970, as Susan Bartlett had a few months before. The new decade belonged to their generation. A year after Woodstock and two before Whitlam, Australian baby boomers plunged into an era that spawned its own anthem, the Skyhooks song *Living in the Seventies*. It caught the mood of the time, an edgy mixture of alienation, self-gratification, sex, drugs and rock 'n' roll. It was a time of full employment and changing social values, and the young and restless could skate from job to job and bed to bed, across the thin ice of a suddenly permissive age.

Some fell through.

The two Sues had been friends from school days at Benalla High in north-eastern Victoria. When Suzanne was 20, in 1969, Susan Bartlett's mother, Elaine Bartlett, had written a reference that read, in part: 'I have known Miss Suzanne Armstrong for five years. She has been a close friend of my daughter Susan since their school days. I know her to be a conscientious and capable young woman.'

Suzanne, oldest of Bill and Eileen Armstrong's four children, raised in farming country at Strathbogie in the hills above Benalla, was intelligent and popular. She found friends and jobs easily, and had plenty of both. She had long brown hair, a good figure and a friendly smile. Men liked her and she liked them.

Whereas Susan Bartlett went teaching, and saved up to travel, Suzanne Armstrong travelled constantly, picking up work and friends as she went. First around Australia and, then, the world — in 1972, and again in 1974, working her way through exotic destinations from South America to South London.

After the second trip she came home with a baby boy, born at Naxos in the Greek islands. The baby's Greek fisherman father had wanted to marry her but the red tape of Greek bureaucracy made marriage difficult and, truth be told, the free-spirited Suzanne was tiring of village life and did not want to be tied to it. Some say she named her son Gregory after a television cameraman who had been a favourite boyfriend before she left, but she often wore a ring with her Greek fiance's name, Manolis, engraved inside it.

Susan Bartlett, who called Suzanne 'little Sue' and was taller and much heavier than her friend, was described by one boyfriend as 'a large girl with a beautiful face.' She had almost married a fellow teacher at Broadford High School, north of Melbourne, in 1973, but had gone overseas on sabbatical leave instead, before returning to teaching, this time in Collingwood.

After Suzanne returned from Greece in 1976 she moved to Collingwood, and picked up a little work minding the baby daughter of a barrister friend, Judith Peirce, whom she had known earlier when she had worked as a courier for Peirce's husband. She rode a bicycle around Carlton and Collingwood, her toddler strapped on a seat behind her. In late October she and Susan Bartlett, who had been in a nearby flat, rented a house together.

It was a neat brick single-fronted Victorian 'one of a pair' of the type even then already popular with inner-suburban renovators. The address was 147 Easey Street, two doors from Hoddle Street. The former school friends were happy, but not for long. Ten weeks later they were dead.

On Tuesday, 11 January, their closest neighbours, Ilona Stevens and Janet Powell, who lived through the shared wall in number 149, found Suzanne Armstrong's part-Labrador pup, Benjy, loose in the street. No-one answered when they knocked next door, so they left a note and took the dog home for safekeeping.

By Thursday morning, 13 January, the note was still in the door and Ilona and Janet's curiosity had overcome their fear of being labelled stickybeaks. They heard little Gregory whimpering, and went down the lane on the other side of number 147, through the open gate and the unlocked back door. Ilona went first.

'I noticed that the kitchen and bathroom lights were on, but none of the others (were) at the back of the house,' she said later. 'In the passage, near the front door, I saw Susan's body. She was lying on her stomach, face down …'

She yelled to her friend, who had paused to look at the note on the kitchen table, to ring the police. Susan was wearing a green nightie.

There was blood down one side, on her legs and on the walls. In the front bedroom, Suzanne's body was on the floor.

'She was lying on her back, legs apart and knees drawn up, and there was a lot of blood... She was naked except for what seemed to be a skivvy pushed up around her neck.'

In the middle bedroom was sixteen-months-old Gregory — dehydrated and distressed and dirty, but alive.

The first job for police was to piece together the dead women's last known movements, and a list of their friends and acquaintances. It was a long list, and it kept them busy. Most murder victims are killed by people who know them, so there were many potential suspects among the men the two Sues knew.

Within days, homicide detectives had gathered what facts they could. They couldn't have guessed that 40 years later, another generation of police wouldn't know much more.

It had happened like this. Suzanne Armstrong had got up early on Monday, 10 January, and shared breakfast with Susan Bartlett before Susan went shopping with her mother at Georges, then Melbourne's elite establishment department store. Mother and daughter lunched together and, according to one account, Mrs Bartlett told her daughter it was time to end 'old associations' and concentrate on new ones — a heavy hint about what she probably saw as both young women's increasingly bohemian lifestyle. After lunch Susan went back to Easey

Street. It was the last time her mother saw her alive.

The two Sues spent the afternoon at home. Susan made a yellow frock to wear on a date with her new boyfriend, a salesman she had met at the Argo Inn in South Yarra. Then she cooked dinner for themselves and her brother Martin Bartlett and his girlfriend, who often visited.

After the meal, the women watched the long-running serial *The Sullivans* while Martin set up a stereo system he'd lent his sister. He and his girlfriend left not long after the show finished at 8.30pm. Later, Suzanne went to bed in the front room, which overlooked Easey Street, and Susan went to bed in the third bedroom, down the hall closer to the kitchen. Gregory was in his cot in the bedroom between. They had never changed their trusting country ways, leaving the back door open and the side gate into the cobbled side lane unlatched. It's possible that oversight proved fatal.

Suzanne was reading a collection of Roald Dahl's short stories, *Switch Bitch*. It seems that something or somebody interrupted her, because it was found, open at the middle pages, on the bed. Detectives who interpreted the scene guessed she put the book down to open the front door because somebody she knew, or thought she knew, came knocking. Either that, or the killer came up the passage from the back door to get to her room, in which case it is more likely that the detectives are right: if a complete stranger had appeared at her bedroom door, already in the house, it seems highly unlikely she would have put the book down so neatly.

But if she got up to answer the front door there is no guarantee it wasn't a stranger knocking. The story she was reading was called The Last Act. For her, it was.

For two full days, no-one knew. Amazingly, three men came into the house during that time but didn't see the bodies at the front of the house and didn't hear the thirsty baby. A fourth man stayed next door on the night of the murder. Each was let go after long interviews, but each was on the suspect list until the DNA tests finally cleared them 21 years later.

Barry Woodard, then 31, was a shearer, a country boy who later grew heartily sick of having his name tossed up every time Easey Street was mentioned. But, at the time, he wasn't shy about his tragically short-lived friendship with Suzanne Armstrong, whom he'd met on a 'blind date' just before Christmas, less than three weeks earlier. They'd had a couple of outings, and had dinner at his sister's place in Northcote the night before she died.

Barry telephoned twice on Monday, evidently when the girls were out, and several times on Tuesday and Wednesday. Puzzled because no-one answered, he and his younger brother, Henry, went to the house about 8.30pm on Wednesday, 12 January, came in the back door and left a note on the kitchen table. Henry wanted to have a look up the darkened hall, but Barry thought it bad manners to be so nosy, so they left.

When news broke the next morning that two women had been found murdered in Collingwood, he rang Easey Street again, from his sister's house. The telephone was engaged, so he assumed the women were safe. But when his sister called the same number five minutes later, a detective answered. Within minutes he, Henry and their sister were picked up, then split up for several hours of intense questioning.

Their stories tallied, but Barry Woodard felt that a question mark hung unjustly over his head for years. Until one afternoon in August 1998, when he came home from work to his house in a country town to find two detectives waiting for him. They asked for a blood sample. He was, like his brother and six other men on that first and overly short list, pleased to give it.

The other man who had been in the house without seeing the bodies was the tobacco salesman who had met Susan Bartlett the previous week. Like the shearer, the salesman was worried because no-one answered his calls, so he drove to Easey Street about 10.30 on Tuesday night

— with a friend, luckily, who was able to verify his story.

After knocking on the front door, he walked down the side lane, climbed through the unlocked window of Susan Bartlett's empty bedroom and copied the house's telephone number on a cigarette packet before climbing back out the window, all without seeing the bodies a few metres up the unlit hall.

The fourth man was the crime reporter named John Grant and known as 'Grunter', one of the hardest of the hard cases working for the then popular and profitable tabloid scandal sheet, *Truth*. Tough, street smart, and with a reputation for wild living that could have got him a job in the armed robbery squad, Grant had 'crashed' for the night in the hallway of Ilona Stevens's house, number 149, on that Monday.

The homicide squad spent a long, hard day questioning Grant but established only that he'd heard nothing through the double brick party wall. What intrigued detectives, and other reporters, was the ghastly coincidence that Grant had also been one of the last people to see Julie Garciacelay, a young American, apparently abducted from her North Melbourne flat in 1975, and almost certainly murdered.

Grant was totally cleared of any involvement in either case but he, too, had to live with innuendo until the DNA tests cleared him. Still wary, perhaps, after his earlier experiences with the law, he had a lawyer with him when he gave his blood sample in 1998.

There were other leads in 1977 — too many, probably — but they all came to nothing. That is, until one of the earliest of them rose to the top of the pile 40 years later.

The knife that Perry Kouroumblis told police he'd found at Victoria Park railway station at 10.30pm on the night of the murders was one of several handed to investigators, including one found on a nearby roof by a roofing contractor.

A man with a history of sex offences was interviewed after stabbing a farmer in Tasmania; he had been living near Collingwood at the time of the murders, and had crossed Bass Strait days later, taking a car with a bloodstained knife, boots and shirt in the boot.

As the police found out, the dead women had known a lot of men who, in turn, knew other men. None of which led to a comprehensive file on possible persons of interest. Two generations of police were amazed at such a tiny file on a double murder. One recalled that it was a few pages in a fragile cardboard manila folder.

The case frustrated the then head of the homicide squad, Detective Inspector Noel Jubb, who was to retire still tormented about what had really happened that night. It also fascinated Tom Prior, a veteran crime reporter and author.

After retiring from daily newspapers in the early 1990s, the irrepressible Prior re-investigated the case to gather material for a book he'd planned for years.

As it happened, Prior was diagnosed with a terminal disease before he finished, and was forced to publish *They Trusted Men* in 1996 knowing it was a work in progress, not the book he'd dreamed of writing.

But the old sleuth made friends with Greg Armstrong, by this time a young man, and helped find his natural father on the Greek island of Naxos, where the two were reunited.

Greg was raised partly by Suzanne's sister, Gayle Tilton, who had a son almost exactly the same age, and partly by Gayle's estranged husband, a farm manager. But the big influence in his life, Prior believes, was his grandmother Eileen, a kindly woman who had remarried after divorcing Bill Armstrong. Bill, too, had married again and moved to a farm near Bairnsdale, but died after being burned fighting a grassfire almost exactly a year after his daughter's murder.

There were other postscripts to Easey Street. One is that, because he was illegitimate, the orphaned boy was not entitled to crime compensation to pay for his rearing and education. That is, until his mother's barrister friend,

Judith Peirce, ran a campaign that resulted in the Premier of the day, Rupert Hamer, changing the law. Judith Peirce set up a trust fund to handle the compensation payment and money donated by members of the public touched by his plight. She used some of the money to send him to boarding school in his teens, leaving the rest in trust to help him through university. His studies include Modern Greek, a language he practised when visiting his new-found father and relatives.

From tragedy, she said once, Greg grew into a remarkable success story. 'He is very much like his mother. Sue was a happy-go-lucky person who could roll with the punches in a way a lot of people can't.'

Tom Prior thought a lot about the case in his last months. For a long time he kept coming back to one name — which, like several others, he changed for legal reasons when writing his book. This is what he wrote of the man he suspected: 'He had had an association with Suzanne Armstrong but claimed he spurned her. He had been to 147 Easey Street and knew the location of the various rooms. He had a violent temper. His marriage had broken down, and a number of previous sexual associations had failed. He had assaulted a woman before. He was known to be drinking at the time of the murders, but had not drunk alcohol for a long time after them. He had given contradictory accounts of his movements during the murder week. And he was not robustly investigated because he was trusted as a former associate of police.'

Prior's hunch seemed as good as any and better than many. But when former Melbourne journalist Helen Thomas decided to write her book on the Easey Street case 20 years later, she was able to pull together a more nuanced and dispassionate account that included some details that would suddenly assume more importance in late September 2024, with the arrest of a former Collingwood man at Rome's international airport.

Once the Italian police had satisfied themselves that Perry Kouroumblis and Periklis Kouroumplis were the same man, he was locked in Rome's notoriously grim prison, Regina Coeli, pending extradition.

What can be said about the accused man is that he was for decades a metal worker who forged and shaped wrought iron at a business in Dandenong. It can also be said that his parents sold their house in Bendigo Street, Collingwood, in July 1977 — the same month as the well-publicised inquest into the deaths of Susan Bartlett and Suzanne Armstrong, at which Kouroumblis's name was raised as the supposed finder of the knife. The parents subsequently moved back to Greece, something that many dual citizens do once after making enough money in Australia to support themselves in relative comfort in their home country. One of Perry's brothers, Andreas or 'Andy', returned to Greece and Perry often visited them there, which is hardly surprising.

What was surprising to cold case detectives was that after they visited Perry Kouroumblis in 2017 to request a DNA sample to eliminate him from their list of 141 names, he went for a 'holiday' to Greece — and did not return. After a near-relative of Kouroumblis was DNA tested to establish a genetic link, his name went on an international watch list.

At the time of going to print, the case against Perry Kouroumblis has quite some way to go. Its ultimate result is by no means a foregone conclusion.

CHAPTER 2
THE HARDER THEY FALL

'First your legs go. Then you lose your reflexes. Then you lose your friends.' – Willie Pep, former boxing champion.

To know how far and how hard Gary Neiwand has fallen, you need to understand how good he was on a racing bike. On the track, he had the lightning reflexes, power and instinct of the born sprinter. Off it, he was the last to leave a party or a pub and the first to pay the bill.

The backslappers loved him – a homegrown world champion who'd buy drinks all night, kid around, attract girls – but it was bound to end in tears. Inside the powerful body of the 'party animal' (his own description), some saw an anxious boy scarred by the pressure that had pushed him to the top.

Finally, he went to jail, a fate that friends and family feared was waiting for him as his life disintegrated after the cheering stopped: a terrible comedown for an athlete who mixed it with the best in the world.

Drugs aside, coaches can't put in what God left out, the saying goes, and the ticket Neiwand drew in the genetic lottery was blistering speed. For a few electrifying seconds, he could spin his legs faster than anyone else on earth. When the field hit the straight and the crowd was on its feet and yelling, the larrikin Australian was odds-on to run down the best sprinters in the game. Even if he'd been out late the night before – which, he admits, he all too often had been.

Neiwand's is a cautionary tale about sporting success and the price some pay for it. It is about the human flaws of a brilliant athlete whose candle burned too brightly – and at both ends. It is about Australia's appetite for winners and a publicly funded system that chews up sporting talent, extracts precious medals and spits out used-up people.

The rise and fall of Gary Neiwand begins in Melbourne's northern suburbs. Like boxing, bike racing was traditionally a working-class sport and the velodromes were in the working-class suburbs north of the Yarra. It was at one of these, the old Northcote track, that the young Neiwand first attracted attention.

It was early 1983. Rik Patterson – son of the Bradman of cycling, multiple world champion Sid Patterson – was then Victorian sprint cycling champion. At 23 years and 88 kilograms, Patterson junior was a gym-honed, all-round athlete in training with the Melbourne Demons

AFL football team. 'I had legs like tree trunks then,' recalls Patterson, now a barrister.

When a battling road rider, a fireman called Ron Neiwand, asked if one of his boys could have a training ride with him, Patterson obliged. He had seen Neiwand senior around the tracks with his tribe of sons. Gary was the second of four, a skinny, strawberry-blond 16-year-old who could have stepped off a skateboard.

The Neiwand boys' mother, Barbara, was sister of a world-class track rider, Clive 'Custard' Middleton. It was from the Middletons they inherited the fast-twitch muscles that make a sprinter. Gary was the pick of the bunch, though there was little reason to know that by looking at him back then.

Patterson remembers 'a kid about five foot six and 60 kilograms' sitting on a battle-scarred track bike handed down by older members of the family.

Any thoughts Patterson had about nursing the youngster vanished after one circuit. The kid went past him as if the state champion were pedalling a postman's pushbike. It took Patterson another circuit to persuade himself what had happened. 'The second time around I was really trying, don't worry about that,' he says wryly. The result was the same. The kid was a speed machine.

Patterson has come to relish telling the story against

himself. It wasn't so amusing then. 'I was totally demoralised,' he laughs. 'That was the moment I decided to give up sprinting and take on the 4000 metres.'

Some riders were more disciplined and consistent than Neiwand, some were better tacticians and some were virtually unbeatable eastern Europeans who took so many steroids they looked like Arnold Schwarzenegger on two wheels.

Neiwand won three world titles and set an Olympic record in a qualifying heat – a record that stood for years – but it is not only the big international races that people remember. Former world champion Gary Sutton, at the height of his own brilliant career when Neiwand started out, says 'every now and then he would just blow you away'.

Sutton first saw Neiwand in an under-17 race at Northcote. 'I watched this kid and asked, "Who's that?" I left my jersey in the dressing room that night and he picked it up and went to give it back to me the next week. I said, "You keep that." He was a good kid.'

Sutton watched Neiwand develop into a rider with explosive speed who frustrated himself and others with his capacity to self-destruct. He won some races with breathtaking ease, but lost some because the pressure got to him.

Once, he says, Neiwand had been moving furniture all day in Adelaide before turning up to race, obviously tired. He admitted to Sutton – who was commentating that night – that he was 'buggered' and had only one fast ride in him.

'He did it in the first race. He was up against Darryn Hill, who was world champion and had just returned from winning a Keirin series in Japan. Gary was an entertainer – he swung into the straight at the back of the bunch waving to the crowd and then let go and got the leader on the line – 'at the death' as we say. He was a lair. He made Darryn Hill and Sean Eadie look like B-grade riders that night.' Hill and Eadie were both Olympians.

Sutton, now New South Wales' head cycling coach and national junior cycling director, loved watching Neiwand. But he and other coaches warn young riders he is a bad example — no-one else can take the liberties he did on and off the track and still win in that whirlwind finish.

Like Shane Warne and the other Gary — the fallen football idol Gary Ablett senior – Neiwand was a natural who could get away with doing things others couldn't, and make it look as easy as a 16-year-old playing against primary school kids. Right up until he couldn't quite do it anymore. That's when the trouble started.

The story broke on 22 May, 2005, and was in most Australian newspapers next morning: Olympic cyclist and former world champion Gary Neiwand had been bailed for $10,000 on charges of breaching an intervention order originally taken out by his estranged wife, Cathy, after 'heated arguments' when they separated in 2001.

In practice, after the first few weeks of their separation, the couple had tacitly ignored the intervention order so their two children could see both parents. They would often have a meal together and Neiwand would visit and sometimes stay at the former family home in Elwood for birthdays and other special occasions. But in early 2005, after three years, the relatively amicable separation turned sour when Cathy Neiwand became friendly with another man, later named in court.

Gary Neiwand blamed this man for 'stirring up trouble' between him and Cathy. Despite his own admitted failings as a husband, he was jealous about what he saw – probably incorrectly – as being usurped as a father figure. (The man concerned strenuously insists he was never more than a friend and did not have a romantic attachment with Cathy Neiwand because he was already in a committed relationship.)

It would have been just another domestic argument except that Neiwand was a high-profile scalp. The media were tipped off and camera crews and reporters were waiting at St Kilda police station when he was charged.

And one bizarre aspect quite naturally pushed the story high on every news list.

The media had been leaked this fact: weeks earlier, an agitated Neiwand had telephoned Cathy and claimed he had entered the backyard while she was hanging out washing and urinated in her champagne glass 'and watched you drink it'. At other times he had abused her for smoking in the house and had yelled, 'Go and sleep with Andrew' when he saw her at their children's school – a reference to what he thought was her new relationship.

It was ugly and acutely embarrassing, but more pathetic than violent. Police would drop all but three of 17 charges laid against Neiwand and he insisted in court (through his barrister) that he had not urinated in the champagne glass at all. But the damage was done.

With a couple of stupid outbursts, a triple world champion and four-time Olympian who had won gold medals at three Commonwealth Games had deservedly made himself despised and derided as a 'stalker'.

It was probably inevitable that some reports likened Neiwand to another Australian cyclist, Stephen Pate, jailed in 2003 for a series of violent attacks on his wife. No-one in cycling was surprised that the thuggish Pate got into trouble but there was, says leading sport commentator Bruce McAvaney, 'a lot of affection for Gary' when he had his first brush with the law. That affection might have faded a little, although many people believe Neiwand needs psychological support.

'I would have named Neiwand and Dean Woods as two pillars of cycling in the 1980s and 1990s,' says McAvaney. 'When I read about it (the charges) I got the shock of my life... I felt very sad for him and his wife.'

The damage to Neiwand was compounded when the charges were heard in late 2005 and the champagne glass story was aired again. Neiwand came to court unshaven and puffy-eyed, wearing a cap and a rugby jumper, and pleaded guilty to two counts of breaching an intervention order and one of criminal damage. It was not a good look for anyone, let alone a former Olympian and one of the world's better athletes.

His barrister Martin Grinberg, a former policeman, did not have to gild the lily to make his point. Here was a man, he told the court, who had fallen into a dark period 'at the end of a career, at the end of a relationship. He finds himself, having been at the absolute pinnacle of his chosen profession, back living with mum and dad and the reality that brings with it'.

Neiwand acknowledged his wrongdoing and made 'an absolute apology' to his ex-wife and children. The apology, perhaps pointedly, did not include the 'other man'. (Despite this, the man later offered to give character evidence in Neiwand's favour.)

The magistrate sentenced Neiwand to a four-month suspended prison term – meaning he would be jailed if he offended again within 18 months, barring exceptional circumstances.

Neiwand might have been remorseful, but the impetuous streak that had caused the trouble soon claimed him again. He made the mistake of speaking when reporters approached him outside court, and found that a 10-second grab under pressure was no way to untangle the causes and effects of a failed marriage.

Pushed for a reaction, he dug a hole for himself by saying he was 'not ashamed' of anything he did. The hole grew deeper when he naively agreed to be interviewed by radio broadcaster Derryn Hinch, setting himself up for a ritual humiliation to titillate the indignation of a talkback audience.

Here was a 39-year-old man, depressed and stressed and probably psychologically disturbed, totally out of his depth and trying to flounder through a nightmare. Even his ex-wife felt sorry for him when she realised he could go to jail. Which, only weeks later, became a distinct probability.

On 24 October, 2005, a Monday morning, two unmarked police cars followed Neiwand's Falcon sedan when he dropped his children at Elwood Primary School after a weekend access visit. Why so many police resources were used was never explained, but it looked as if someone saw Neiwand as a trophy, perhaps as a public relations move to show the force was tough on 'domestics', which is an understandable strategy.

Neiwand drove down St Kilda Street, a main road, towards cafes where, he claimed later, he was hoping to have a coffee with other cyclists who gather there after training rides. He did nothing unusual and the police did not pull him over, but they arrested him later that day because his estranged wife lived in St Kilda Street. He had breached the intervention order by driving past the house, the one he had bought with money he won racing in Japan in 1994. A lot had changed in a decade.

After the police charged him, he went home to his parents' house in West Essendon and swallowed half a bottle of sleeping tablets and some Valium. He then 'sent a lot of messages' and became unconscious.

An old friend, Troy Tyler, got there in time and made sure he woke up.

For Neiwand, Tyler is a reminder of what might have been if he hadn't been born with the fast-twitch muscles that created tough choices others didn't have to make.

At 40, Tyler now counts himself lucky he wasn't a great

bike rider like his troubled mate. When he and Neiwand first met as teenagers in a novice race, he says, 'I knew I was always going to be a club race rider and Gary was going to be a superstar.' For a long time, he envied Neiwand's talent. Recently, he found out that Neiwand envied him his normal life – and for good reason.

While Neiwand trained full-time with the Australian Institute of Sport in Adelaide, Tyler did a carpentry apprenticeship. Later, he joined a transport company and bought his first house, renovated and sold it. Now a manager, he has just 'traded up' to his third house. He is prosperous and content for himself – but angry that his mate, after half a lifetime at the top of world cycling, was left stranded.

'After the 2000 Games, Gary was like a 16-year-old in the workforce because he didn't have anything to fall back on,' says Tyler. 'He was going to be too old (for the next Olympics), so everyone dropped him like a hot potato. What he'd done didn't matter anymore. There was no gold watch, no thank you, no recognition and no job. He'd won a silver medal at his fourth Olympics and he didn't even get an interview in the paper.'

Tyler conceded his friend has been 'a bit of a rogue who bucked the system' but he didn't criticise him too much. Few people did, beyond pointing out that Neiwand was his own worst enemy. There was not much point kicking a man who was already down – and who is his own toughest critic.

The late, great George Best, a soccer hero who became a tragic story of self-destruction, tops a long list of gifted sportsmen who drank themselves onto skid row. Waiting for Neiwand in a Footscray café, you wonder if he is a candidate for the same club.

When Neiwand made his last brave ride at the Sydney Olympics he was 80 kilograms of muscle. When he walks into the café five years later, Neiwand the civilian is 96 kilograms but looks strongly built rather than overweight. Of middle height, he has the loaded shoulders and thighs of the power athlete, moves quickly and has a strong grip.

He has pale blond hair, red stubble and bright green eyes, bloodshot from lack of sleep. At the time, he was working late shift as 'evening supervisor' in a West Melbourne warehouse – 'a forklift driver with a title,' he quips drily, but doesn't laugh. When he gets home to his parents' house after midnight he mostly plays internet poker until dawn, then gets a few hours in bed before lunch and the start of another shift. Not a great life, but better than some of the alternatives. Being busy cuts down time to brood.

In Sydney, he went within 'a tyre width' of winning the Keirin after leading all the way. He was beaten on the line by Florian Rousseau, multiple Olympic medallist and one of the best sprinters in history. If Neiwand had won gold at 34 at his fourth Games, fans would have ranked it near Kieren Perkin's stirring 1500-metre swim at Atlanta or with Bill Roycroft riding with a broken collarbone at Rome in 1960. But he didn't and it haunts him. In his mind, it had been his chance to make up for missing gold in Atlanta four years before.

Neiwand came home from Sydney and fell apart. All he had to show for 17 years riding against the world's best were two bikes in his car boot – and the Australian Institute of Sport had demanded one of them back, in the only telephone call he received from the institute. It was a bitter end to what he saw as a wasted career. Within months he had – for the second time in five years – separated from his wife, this time with two children. 'It wasn't Cathy's fault,' he says. 'I couldn't live with myself and so it was hard for her.' He left, but the hollow feeling followed.

In that first year, his weight shot to 112 kilograms. A diet of pub parmigianas, vodka and lemonade and self-loathing will do that. He had moved into a dilapidated house in Hawthorn owned by a friend, AFL footballer Ben Dixon. He ate and drank at the nearby Beehive Hotel until the money ran out. Then he started working there.

When a new licensee, Kevin Hannett, took over the pub in late 2001, he was astonished to find one of Australia's greatest sportsmen washing dishes. Hannett made Neiwand a barman and then night manager so he could afford to move out of the old house 'because the roof was falling in and he couldn't take his kids there'.

Things looked up. Neiwand got a better house and Cathy and the children visited. The hotel job suited him because the rule was that if you were on duty you didn't drink. This changed when Neiwand took a new job selling real estate just as the market slowed: he was entertaining clients but sales were down and the drinking was up. It didn't last.

He moved to his parents' house in Essendon to save money – but all that did, he admits, was let him spend more on 'partying'. Then his fragile world fell apart when he believed that his estranged wife took up with another man, and he could no longer see his children so freely. The intervention order they had tacitly ignored for three years had to be obeyed or the police would come. He was jealous, angry and confused and did very stupid things.

He had lost the Olympic races he wanted most, then he lost his marriage, and he lost the plot.

Sport, like life itself, is littered with casualties. In a suburban TAB agency walking distance from the pub where Neiwand worked, a former champion footballer – a premiership player – can often be seen betting desperately on every race. In a country pub in north-east Victoria, a lean little man who rode Melbourne Cup winners drinks with one hand, and smokes and feeds a poker machine with the other.

Neither will ever recapture the rich addictive mixture of adrenaline and adulation they felt on some long-ago afternoons. But, like a thousand others, they will go on trying to fill the gap.

And Neiwand? In early 2006, he still had a chance to step back from the brink. One of his best chances was to listen to John Beasley, the cycling coach he had turned to when he came home from Adelaide in 1998 after arguments with national coaches that stopped him competing in the 1999 world championships.

Then, Beasley took Neiwand back to grass roots, training him at the old Northcote track with a few keen youngsters and rekindling his love of the sport so that he went to the Sydney Games as fit as he had been in a decade. 'We did the hard work, but without anyone holding a gun at my head,' Neiwand was to say of Beasley's light touch.

Beasley, a former track rider whose Footscray bike shop is the hub of a cycling dynasty spanning four generations, sees Neiwand as a casualty of a 'medal factory' syndrome. 'To measure success only by gold medals is pretty sad,'

Beasley says. 'For the last couple of decades, I think athletes have come out of the system absolutely destroyed.'

Beasley practises what he preaches. He coaches a team – the Drapac Porsche squad – aimed at 'balancing work, personal and sporting lives' to allow for the fact that when athletes retire, they still have two-thirds of their lives to live.

Neiwand's main problem, he says, is that in all the years he was coached, nothing prepared him for the first day of the rest of his life. But at least now he is talking about it.

Friends warned Neiwand to be wary of the media – understandably, given what had happened – but he was frank in telling the inside story of his life and what he calls 'wasted years'.

As a youngster, he was keener on cricket and football than cycling, but the day came when he followed his father and older brother onto the bikes.

When he won his first race, the die was cast.

He left school – 'Niddrie Tech' in Melbourne's north-western suburbs – in his mid-teens and worked for a signwriter for a while, still playing cricket and football and competing in junior bike races. He had just begun an apprenticeship with the signwriter and been asked to train with the Essendon under-19 football squad when he was offered a place in what would become the Australian Institute of Sport cycling program in Adelaide.

Neiwand was 18. He left home, gave up his apprenticeship and didn't work again until he was almost double that age, although he drew a salary for years under a sponsorship deal with Carlton United Breweries set up by the company's then chief Peter Bartels, a former international cyclist who effectively became his patron.

Neiwand is grateful the sponsorship helped support him but bitter about the AIS, which he now sees as 'buying' success at the expense of sometimes vulnerable young athletes.

'My whole time at the institute was a farce,' he says. 'I'd encourage any young rider now to stay at home. I should have stayed home, but I knew that if I didn't go there I wouldn't get the good bikes and equipment. And at the back of your mind is the possibility of not being selected.'

He describes living in a rented AIS house, only loosely supervised, with other young riders who divided their time between training and looking for a good time. The pattern was to train, sleep, get up and go out to pubs and nightclubs then snatch a little sleep to sober up for more training: setting a pattern of adolescent misbehaviour that was hard to break, later.

When riders weren't training in Adelaide, they were travelling for weeks or months at a time, competing around the world. Riding the track circuit overseas was like touring in a rock band: boredom building to bouts of intense activity followed by the urge to let off steam.

The main recreations were those of soldiers on leave: sex, drinking, drugs and gambling.

One former Australian rider, still heavily connected with cycling, says (on condition of anonymity) most people would be shocked by the life of track riders touring overseas. 'Racing in circuits is a bit surreal anyway and racing in other countries is like going away to a war. You live like a single guy, rooting everything that moves. If my kids knew some of the things I did – well, it was just crap. It's not a natural lifestyle.'

Young riders could even be led astray by coaches and officials, says another retired rider who competed overseas in the 1980s. At his first international race meeting in Britain, a well-known Australian official invited him to watch 'movies' with other riders.

'I assumed the movies would be motivational. But the first image I saw was of a naked black man with a German shepherd dog. Pornography – that was my introduction to (official's name). He was a nasty piece of work. His idea of humour was to blow up his foreskin with a bike pump. It was well-known he was a big amphetamine taker back when he raced.'

Neiwand confirms such stories but admits he could find

trouble without any help from others. 'I am not proud of the majority of what I've done,' he says. 'I was a coach's and a wife's worst nightmare.'

They call track riders 'boxers on wheels'. Outside the boxing ring, sprint cycling is probably the most aggressive Olympic sport. Neiwand says he was always willing 'to risk losing skin' to win a race. He knows about head butts and elbows and putting riders 'over the fence' – and he learned early to never show he was hurt.

But no matter how well he plays tough guy, two subjects make his eyes glisten. One is his failure as a husband. The other is his perception he failed as an Olympic cyclist. The two are linked.

Neiwand first met Cathy McCartin in 1989. She worked for Carlton United Brewery's public relations division and was his day-to-day contact at the firm. He asked her to a formal dinner in Melbourne and began an attachment that eventually became a long engagement. They married in 1994, their son was born the following year and a daughter four years later.

Cathy's workmates privately wondered whether it was wise for the warm, friendly woman they knew to marry an intense sportsman who had to tour overseas so much. 'Gary was an achiever but not a happy person,' recalls one senior colleague. 'I saw a darkness there and wondered how Cathy would cope.'

Neiwand admits he was 'three quarters' to blame for problems in the marriage. 'I was more than happy with Cathy and I don't regret marrying because we have got the two best kids in the world – but, really, I shouldn't have got married. I led two lives – one with her and one with cycling. I shouldn't have exposed someone to the party lifestyle I wasn't willing to leave.'

One of his happiest memories is of the world titles in Norway in 1993, when Cathy flew in to watch him. They had a big night out the night before an important heat. 'I was dry retching in the middle of the ground before the race,' he recalls. But he survived it, went and had 'a sleep and a steak' and that night he beat the German powerhouse sprinter Michael Hubner to win one of two world titles he took home from that trip.

It was all or nothing. When he didn't win big races he wanted, he sank into depression masked by defiance, alcohol and anything else that might distract him.

At Atlanta in 1996, he set an Olympic record in a qualifying heat but missed getting into the ride-off for the gold medal. He started drinking before the ride-off for third and fourth, effectively handing the bronze medal to the Canadian Curtis Harnett, who had not beaten him before.

John Beasley blames such over-reactions on an artificial

environment that warped judgment. Whereas previous generations of athletes had jobs and trained around work, the emphasis on 'professionalism' in Neiwand's era disconnected athletes from home, family and workday life, and gave them too much spare time.

They were cocooned in an unreal world in which only sport mattered – one in which losing becomes a kind of death. And in which the reward for winning was to be treated like a spoilt child, teaching 'winners' not to take responsibility for their own actions.

Neiwand now sees the game more clearly. He is wistful rather than bitter, a man with a broken heart. 'I don't want to see another kid with potential throw away his life like I threw mine away, trying to achieve something I didn't achieve.'

He thinks about what might have been. He mentions the film *Sliding Doors* with its tantalising premise that just one different move along the way would change a life. Once he dreamed of medals, fame and fortune.

Now his fantasy is that the 18-year-old Neiwand closed the door on full-time cycling and stayed home instead and played football and cricket, turned a job into a career and raced bikes as a hobby. 'By now I'd be a happily married normal human being,' he says. 'Instead of a fly-by-the-pants party boy – a Philippoussis with no money.'

Less than a year after he said that, it's too late to mend bridges, let alone broken hearts. He was back on talking terms with Cathy for a while and both were happy about it for the children's sake. She told the author in early 2006 she didn't want her children's father to go to jail because it would serve no purpose. She said he loved his children and would never do anything to hurt them. She was glad he appeared to have escaped from 'the horrible place he was in' a few months before that. Sadly, she was wrong.

Gary Sutton, still New South Wales state coach, always thought that Neiwand had plenty to offer. He tells the story of asking him to Narrabeen in 1995 as a guest speaker. After Neiwand spoke, Sutton offered him the agreed appearance fee, but he handed it back. 'He said, "There's a kid out there with a red bike – he needs a new set of wheels. Use the money to buy him one".' Sutton did as he was asked, but the boy never heard the truth about where his new racing bike came from because Sutton knew Neiwand would not want to hurt the battling family's pride.

Later, says Sutton, that kid became one of the best riders in the national squad. Last March, Neiwand wasn't invited to the Commonwealth Games despite the fact he was a triple gold medallist. In fact, he was lucky not to be in jail when the Games were on. At the last minute, he was offered a ticket by a kind-hearted person and so got to watch the kid he helped to ride for Australia.

If there were happy endings in real-life sporting fairytales, going to the Games would have been a turning point for the troubled cyclist. Instead, he slid further into depression and erratic, frightening behaviour.

Before being jailed in late 2006 for breaching the intervention order taken out by his wife, he re-offended – with another woman. He was jailed for a total of 18 months, and ordered to serve a minimum of nine months after pleading guilty in the Melbourne Magistrates Court to five charges of stalking, two of theft, three of using a carriage service in a harassing manner and one of breaching an intervention order.

The court was told he had started making 'hang-up' calls to the home and mobile phones of a woman after she broke up with him. After the woman changed her phone numbers, he started making hang-up phone calls to her mother and sent sexually explicit text messages about the woman to her boss.

Chief Magistrate Ian Gray said the offences were serious and a clear message needed to be sent that such conduct was unacceptable. But he said he accepted that Neiwand was suffering depression at the time and was experiencing difficulties with his marriage break-up.

Before he was taken to jail, Neiwand said he hoped it

would give him a chance to get fit so that he could start again by coaching young riders. Time will tell.

In 2007 Neiwand joined the Sunrise Foundation set up by former AFL footballer Wayne Schwass to tackle depression. In December 2011 Neiwand pleaded guilty to two charges of wilful and obscene exposure in Melbourne. These offences occurred after he had been released on a court order in December 2010 on unrelated charges, and was ordered to attend Forensicare and counselling about his behaviour. The court heard that Neiwand had attended counselling, had his drinking problems under control and was upset about his offending and his predicament. The magistrate adjourned the case until March 2012, when he was sentenced to four months jail, wholly suspended for two years.

CHAPTER 3
THE SHOOTIST

He's extremely cunning, very patient and very, very deadly – note in Billy Longley's police file.

On the waterfront they called it the 'apple cucumber' but it wasn't health food. It was gangster slang for a deadly double cross that works like this: a false friend lures the target to a meeting that turns into an ambush when a third party arrives, armed and unannounced. That's the sneaky way they nearly got Billy 'The Texan' Longley in 1971. But he was too smart for them.

Longley got a call from Alfred 'The Ferret' Nelson, social secretary of the painters and dockers union, a job description that covered a lot of ground. Nelson asked Longley to meet him in the Webb Dock mess room, where waterfront workers sometimes ate their lunch and always minded their own business, even if they happened to get spattered with blood.

Longley had to sit with his back to the swinging doors because his host was already seated, facing him across the long mess table. Longley gently slid his handgun out of his belt and, as they chatted about union business, aimed it underneath the table at Nelson. In his business, it was insurance.

The small talk stopped when Longley heard the doors swish behind him. He cocked the hidden pistol and turned to see who was coming. It wasn't good. Jack Twist, famed on the docks for croaking the notorious standover man Freddy 'The Frog' Harrison years before, was approaching fast. He had his hands deep in his overalls pockets and a look on his face that said he had a gun in each of them.

This, Longley observed later with studied understatement, was 'a fairly serious situation.'

But Longley had an advantage: Nelson had heard him cock the gun and realised any hostile move by Twist meant getting shot. 'When I cocked my piece "The Ferret" went white,' Longley was to recall. 'He was a nano-second from death. He said "Bill! Give me a chance – let me talk to him" and he got up and ran up to Twist and threw his arms around him so he couldn't get his guns out of his pockets. Then he took him outside. I should have shot 'em both then and there,' he adds in disgust. Time hasn't dulled some old hatreds.

'The Ferret' saved himself that day – but not for long. He disappeared from his Collingwood lodging soon after, just before the painters and dockers union election in December 1971 that erupted into an open gunfight, a public battle in a long-running guerrilla war in which perhaps dozens of 'dockies' died and many more were injured.

Police were to winch Nelson's car from the water near South Wharf but he was not in it. Much later, a detective standing on a new concrete ramp on the dock was told 'Watch it, you're standing on "The Ferret".' Nelson's body was never found. But there was no doubt, as Longley deadpanned later, that he had 'given up smoking and drinking.' And he wasn't the only one on the missing list.

'It was self preservation,' Longley says, quiet but unrepentant. 'Get in first, before they get you.'

So much for Longley the gunslinger. What about the man? He is rather more complicated. He has been a pigeon fancier, skilled tradesman, bull-mastiff dog breeder, ballroom dancer, committed unionist, hack golfer and handy tennis player, a patient father to his only daughter and grandfather to her children.

Accused (and later convicted) of shooting a painters and dockers union secretary, he had the cunning and the contacts to hide from his underworld enemies and police for sixteen months before turning himself in. He had the willpower to give up smoking in jail – and to lose 30 kilograms at Weight Watchers after getting out. He had the personality to partner a former policeman to persuade delinquent teenagers to mend their ways and errant debtors to pay their way. He reads military histories, biographies and *The Age* newspaper and plays Scrabble.

And lately, every morning, he does water aerobics with a group of respectable older women who won't hear a bad word about their Bill.

Times change. In the 1950s, Longley's favourite water sport was tossing beer cans in the Murray River and shooting them with a pistol as they floated past. He made himself a good shot – one reason he grew old when so many of his contemporaries didn't.

'I've had blokes miss me with six shots from two car lengths away,' he recalls. 'But I didn't miss many.' He almost smiles.

Because of the dockers' code of silence most such incidents were never made public. But one showdown was later aired in court. It happened on a Saturday night in July 1968 at the Rose and Crown Hotel in Port Melbourne after one John Robert Waymouth made the mistake of abusing Billy's partner, Barbara, after accidentally bumping her.

Waymouth was grabbed from behind by several willing hands and tossed out of the bar and onto the street. He was given a belting and left in the gutter as a lesson in etiquette. When Waymouth revived, he made another mistake: he wanted revenge. He called his two sons, who turned up with three friends to even the score.

In the ensuing brawl, guns were produced. At least, one gun was – the one that did all the damage. The result was that five men ended up with .45 calibre bullet wounds, mostly in the buttocks. Two of them decided not to press charges.

Longley heard that the police wanted to question him over the shooting of three men. Five days later he presented himself – with his lawyer, the legendary Frank Galbally – at South Melbourne police station. He was charged on three counts apiece of wounding with intent to murder and grievous bodily harm.

The case against him looked strong but it soon sprang leaks. For a start, only Waymouth was willing to claim that Longley had fired the shots. The other witnesses, including the wounded, seemed unsure what had happened. One even said he did not think Longley had fired the shots.

The clincher came from the courtroom genius of 'The Silver Fox', Galbally, who smoothly led Waymouth into the trap of admitting that the police had shown him a picture of Longley in their efforts to identify him as the shooter. There was, as Galbally and the judge knew, a legal precedent that unless a witness had selected a picture of the supposed guilty party from several photographs of different people, it was inadmissible. The case was dismissed. And another chapter in the intertwined stories of the legendary lawyer and his valued client, Billy Longley, became lore.

For a long time after that, if Galbally had any problems in his chambers with cranky clients or bad debtors, Longley would drop in and sort it out. 'If ever I had a hurdle to jump, I always went to Mr Frank,' he said later. 'He protected me from the slings and arrows.'

They called him 'The Texan' because, the story goes, he wore a big Stetson hat and carried a Colt .45 pistol. Longley disputes this. 'The hat wasn't that big,' he growls, face as sombre as a well-kept grave.

In fact, the nickname came from a TV western series, *The Texan*, made from 1958 to 1960, when Longley was a towering figure on the waterfront, feared nearly as much in Sydney as he was in Melbourne. The show starred a laconic hero coincidentally called Bill Longley, who wouldn't be pushed around by bad guys and was polite to women folk: an irresistible role model for a well-dressed man about town who liked dancing and shooting.

'The Texan' is 80 now, one of few to survive the Melbourne dock wars that, as he points out with a historical flourish, inflicted more casualties than the Eureka Rebellion – around 40 men dead and many more wounded during a decade that spawned the now-notorious saying, 'We catch and kill our own.'

The Federated Painters and Dockers Union was a closed shop, harder to get into than The Melbourne Stock Exchange. Members joined by invitation based on their reputation. Longley, a wharfie for 17 years, became a 'dockie' in 1967. Of around 360 members, 200 had serious criminal records.

It was only natural, he says, that men with criminal records who could not get jobs elsewhere would end up in the few jobs where a record was not held against them. It was self-selection. Longley's friend, the feared former policeman Brian Murphy, points out that there was a Vagrancy Act in those days, which meant that anyone without a job or visible means of support could be thrown in jail at the whim of police and magistrates. One answer to that was to join a waterside union, therefore getting on the roster for casual work.

Not that it was easy to get a job on the Melbourne wharves. In his book, Longley describes a remarkable scene of working class history:

You went and appeared at the West Melbourne stadium (Festival Hall) where all the fights took place and you walked on the stage under the arc lights in front of all these blokes so that they could take a look at you. You were tested for soundness, and if you were undesirable they might yell out 'YOU! You bludger – you repossessed my sister's refrigerator, you rotten bastard!' They didn't want undesirables – so if you were a police informer, a child molester or a debt collector you didn't stand a chance. You'd be booed out of the hall and the union and be lucky, as the saying went, 'to escape with your ears'. You'd have to come pretty well recommended to get a job on the wharves – they were men's men, the cream of the crop.

Not that Longley had any trouble with scrutiny under the bright lights at the 'House of Stoush'. Having passed muster with his peers, he was warned by the chairman of the Stevedoring Industry Board that he was 'on probation' because of his police record.

'Don't think you're coming down here to steal, fight or be playing up in any way,' the chairman warned him on his first day. Longley assured him he was just after a steady job. It is true that in the next three decades he was not always a stranger to stealing and fighting. But along the way he made lifelong friends with many ordinary wharfies who were not criminals, but working-class men supporting their families the best way they could. Such friendships with 'cleanskins' would save his life later, when he 'went into smoke' to avoid both the police and his enemies in the rival painters and dockers faction.

Longley was invited to be a painter and docker in 1967. It was, he knew, because he had a reputation as a 'gunnie' that would be useful to those who sponsored him into the union. Men like him were insurance for union organisers who did not want to be pushed around.

The reality was that there was a quiet but deadly war between rival groups of gangsters intent on controlling the union and, therefore, lucrative rackets such as 'ghosting' (picking up pay packets for non-existent workers), systematic pilfering and smuggling. Some 'dockies' also indulged in armed robbery, illegal gambling and standover rackets. Whoever controlled the docks effectively controlled organised crime in Australia.

Later, in 1980, an exposé by *The Bulletin* magazine led to the Costigan royal commission into waterfront corruption, which exposed rackets that had tentacles reaching into every level of society – from drug running to illegal gambling and, notably, 'bottom-of-the-harbour' tax rorts exploited by supposedly legitimate business people.

Longley was no angel, and liked easy money as much as the next gunman, but unlike a lot of career criminals he had been a genuine worker and was proud of it: he had served an apprenticeship as a tradesman and had spent his formative years working in industry, as had his father.

He has never wavered from his claim that when he stood as union president in December 1971 it was on a genuine reform ticket to protect ordinary members. In his view, then and later, the battlers who did the dirty, dangerous work on the docks were sold out by greedy union leaders willing to enrich themselves by doing corrupt deals with shipping lines.

Longley has always insisted he won the vote – one of the vote counters told him he'd 'shit it in' – but, after a gun battle, the ballot box was stolen and voting slips were destroyed. This outrage rankled and almost certainly led to his brave and perhaps foolhardy decision ultimately to brief the journalist who wrote the *Bulletin* exposé and, subsequently, to give evidence to the Costigan commission about the rackets that would eventually lead to the union being deregistered in 1993.

But that was later.

Despite the Hollywood nickname, Longley is a reminder of a vanished Australia: the sort of man once seen at RSL clubs and in the betting ring at the races, shaped by 1930s austerity, stern Victorian forebears and a predominantly Anglo-Celtic society.

At a glance, he could be any respectable retired grandfather. He would not look out of place at the Lions Club, on a racing club committee, even in church. When he goes out, he wears a dark suit, white shirt and perfectly knotted tie, and gleaming black shoes. Fingernails clean and clipped. Grey hair combed. He always had presence. Dignity, even.

He has none of the stereotype markers of the criminal underclass: no tattoos, little jewellery, no addiction to gambling, alcohol or drugs. He is gruff but not rough, with a courtliness few would mistake for weakness.

If he were ever a swashbuckler that has long gone; now he looks somewhere between Alfred Hitchcock and the old gunfighter played by John Wayne in his last film, *The Shootist*, doing what a man has to do before the final ride to Boot Hill. There are a few waiting for him there. It has been said for 30 years that Longley was the last to see several of his waterfront opponents alive; legend suggests as many as 15.

Certainly, his lawyers once told him police threatened to charge him with seven murders. Longley vehemently denies any part of killing painters and dockers union secretary Pat Shannon in 1973 – for which he was later jailed – but is quiet about other deaths. To be fair, he is silent about most things from his past. He speaks only when he has something to say, sticking grimly to a code of silence that, at his age, has all but lost its relevance.

Most of the stories he could tell would be about dead men, as he has virtually outlived his generation of crims and knockabouts, dockies and wharfies, and a group of tough and corrupt police who used fists, handcuffs and guns to extract their dues from the underworld in the name of law and order.

He says his fearsome reputation was 'like wearing a hair shirt', though he concedes it had some advantages. For instance, it might have saved his life in jail – though it probably put him there in the first place.

Dead men tell no tales and for most of his life, neither has Longley. Once, his idea of a long sentence was 13 years for murder – which is the time he served over the Shannon shooting. But since agreeing to a book about his life (his biography *In Your Face* was launched in July 2005) he is warming to the talking business. Sometimes he puts several sentences together. But not often.

'I get sick of talking about myself,' he told the authors in a frank moment. 'It shits me.' In the past, in his line of work, silence suited him. He found Teddy Roosevelt's injunction – to speak softly and carry a big stick – more effective.

At his 80th birthday dinner at the Royal Hotel in Essendon, the new talkative Billy Longley spoke for at least three minutes. Perhaps two. 'I look around and see good faces, kind faces,' he began gravely, as his only daughter Lisa took snaps of the eclectic gathering. 'I only mix with good people these days.'

He mentioned several guests by name – starting with his biographer, journalist Rochelle Jackson, a policeman's daughter who first met him while researching a television current affairs story a decade ago, and started on the book in 2003. Another guest was a retired Pentridge prison governor, Jim Armstrong, who later told the crowd that in jail Longley 'was a straight stick in a pile of debris' and a man who 'walked his own line'.

Longley says he has 'Catholic tastes' in friends as well as interests, a point underlined by the gathering at his birthday. Playing the violin and leading the singing at the party was a former journalist who advises the Liberal Party on tactics and policy. Singing along was Dean Mighell, hard-nosed leader of the Electrical Trades Union, who grew up in the northern suburbs knowing the Longley legend.

Other guests included Brian Francis Murphy, a renowned former policeman who became friendly with Longley after refusing to give trumped-up evidence against him over the shooting of five men in the Rose and Crown Hotel. After Longley left prison in 1988, Murphy joined him in a troubleshooting mediation business with the motto 'everything can be negotiated.' Their specialty was debt collecting and persuading wayward teenagers to avoid a life of crime. They were considered most persuasive. Often a business card in a letter box was enough to bring a speedy resolution to problems.

Also at the birthday party was one of Billy's brothers,

Reg Longley, looking the respectable retired barber he is in reefer jacket, cardigan and spectacles. Others included the couple who ran the Moonee Ponds coffee shop where Longley sat at the same table for years, greeting a stream of friends most mornings. For a long time the couple knew the polite older man only as 'Bill' and didn't realise his notoriety until his picture was in the newspaper one morning. Then they understood why so many older locals – men and women – came in and shook hands or kissed him. He was the Godfather of Puckle Street.

The café has changed hands recently, and Longley has switched allegiance to another one in Ascot Vale, around the corner from his flat.

Phillip Adams – broadcaster, film-maker, columnist, stirrer – didn't get to Billy's birthday party. He now only occasionally corresponds with Longley, but his observations of the man he sometimes visited in prison 25 years ago are still vivid. Adams, then an *Age* columnist, received thousands of letters a year but he sensed a powerful personality in a note Longley wrote to him from Pentridge in the late 1970s. That – and, he cheerfully admits, Longley's notoriety – drew him to visit and to write to him and about him. He did, after all, have a column to fill and Longley needed a voice in the world outside jail, so they suited each other's purposes. Something they both recognise in each other.

Adams was streetwise enough to be wary of being manipulated by 'a highly intelligent man'. But at his first sight of Longley, in a security cage used for prison visits in Pentridge's H division, he was struck by 'this charming, likable avuncular gentleman with all this violence swirling around him like a mist'. Curious, Adams asked barrister friends about Longley's conviction for Shannon's murder 'and the consensus was he didn't do it but had done plenty of others'.

It was the beginning of an odd friendship between the cultured and affluent intellectual and a middle-aged gunman surviving in a prison system where any one of many younger men might have killed him for reputation or reward. Longley had his ways of surviving. One was to mind his own business, and to let the mystique that had grown around him work its effect. He gave no offence but he gave the impression that anyone who interfered with him was 'in for seven years bad luck, that's for sure'.

Often, as a billet trusted to mop floors in Pentridge, he was called on to mop up blood spilt after officers 'flogged' a prisoner with batons. A senior officer quietly said to him one day, 'This won't happen to you, will it Bill? We know you'd even up.' It was a case of the reputation that put him inside protecting him while he was there. A double-edged sword.

Reputation wasn't quite enough. Longley's strong personality helped him get what he wanted. He once persuaded Phillip Adams to drive to Ararat prison, two hours from Melbourne, to give him a set of golf clubs. When Adams saw him there he was reminded of 'an old caged lion living carefully' among younger prisoners. What he didn't know was that the old lion still had teeth: he had a pistol stashed inside the jail, just in case.

The funny thing was, years later Longley was talking to a retired prison officer who told him the prison staff had known he had a pistol hidden somewhere.

Adams says he has interviewed possibly 20,000 people 'and I forget most of them before they're out of the room – but I've never forgotten Billy'. He was intrigued by what he calls 'the cognitive dissonance between what he did and the sort of rather sweet guy he seemed to be'.

Adams was describing Longley as he was in his 50s. At 80, the dissonance between the dignified old man and his menacing reputation is even more striking. For his birthday, Longley dressed in Sunday best – conservative grey suit, white shirt, muted tie, polished shoes. He is not tall and his stocky figure has ballooned recently because ageing legs no longer allow him to play golf or tennis or follow his lifelong passion for ballroom dancing. His hands are manicured. In dress and manner he could be a retired country bank manager at a family wedding. Almost.

The only hint of his past is a hard streak, like an old army sergeant who has seen battle and is used to command. Which, had things been slightly different, he might have been.

He was born in 1925, second son and fourth child of eight belonging to Wilfred and Elizabeth Longley, who had arrived in Australia after World War I just in time for the Depression. He says he was christened 'Billy' rather than 'William' because it was his mother's pet name for her favourite brother.

Wilfred Longley was a Yorkshire man, a fitter and turner who had served as a Navy petty officer in the war and had married up the social scale when he wed Elizabeth Holbest Roxburgh, a Scottish school teacher from the Isle of Lewis, and daughter of a naval commander. If Elizabeth had hoped Australia promised something better than a bleak Scottish island for her growing family, she was disappointed. Wilfred had to chase work, sometimes interstate, while she coped with a series of mean rented houses in Melbourne's working-class West.

When Longley says the Depression and poverty pushed him into a life of crime, a listener can tell he's sung the same song so often he might even believe it himself. As with most beliefs, it must have sprung from a grain of truth. But he admits that his surviving siblings (two sisters died in childhood, an emotional scar he avoids talking about) grew up as respectable 'square-heads', embarrassed by his lawlessness. To hear him interpret his own life story, it seems that hardship sharpened a rebellious streak in him that his brothers and sisters did not have. He fought for survival and begged and stole to eat as a boy, then got to like it.

He traces his hatred of authority to the day a conductor kicked him in the face as he clung to the side of the tram for a free ride. 'My face hit the tram track and I skidded along, finishing in a bloody mess.' He recalls a passing motorist picking him up, bleeding, from the gutter and taking him home.

There were other turning points. He remembers the day his father got into a brawl with a neighbour and was being badly beaten. 'I ran to the toolbox and grabbed a hammer and hit him (the other man) in the kidneys as hard as I could,' says Longley. Then he hit him in the head. Although his father preached 'tact and diplomacy' to his sons, his actions sent a different message. He took the boy to a pub, rewarded his loyalty with praise, oysters and porter gaff. And so he learned at an impressionable age that violence paid off – a lesson hard to unlearn.

Longley clearly loved his mother, and inherited her love

of reading, but he admits evading her efforts to steer him away from trouble. From the little he says, and much he doesn't, emerges a picture of a worn-out and homesick woman, disappointed by her lot, heartbroken at the loss of two daughters and the lack of opportunity for her other children. Longley doesn't criticise his father, but the implication is clear: it wasn't a happy household.

On Sundays, he says, he would suggest that his mother read in bed while he cooked a roast dinner for the family. She quoted poetry to him that he can still recite a lifetime later and she told him he was 'fey' – had the intuition of her Celtic forebears. He believed this sixth sense saved his life, later. But it didn't keep him out of trouble.

He was expelled from Ascot Vale primary school in sixth grade for punching a teacher who threatened to strap his younger sister, Peggy.

He had already been in trouble for stealing cigarettes from a shop. In early 1937, he got 12 months probation for shoplifting. In late 1938, he was sent to a boys' home for attempted shop breaking.

By the time he got out, war was looming and employment booming. The Depression was over. His father started work at the ordnance factory at Maribyrnong and got him a fitting and turning apprenticeship. Young Billy liked work. It might have been a stabilising influence but any harmony was shattered when his mother's father fell ill in Britain; despite the war, Mrs Longley got a passage 'home' to nurse the old navy man.

Billy was 15, and scared his mother might not get back. He describes how the family stood on the dock, crying, as her ship steamed away. They watched it until it became a dot and disappeared over the horizon. It was the end of his childhood.

Billy and two of the other children went to board with other families and his father looked after the other three. He was treated well and speaks fondly of the family he stayed with, but adolescence was not a good time to be missing his mother's influence.

He bought a shotgun from a workmate, took up rabbit shooting and fantasised about what he would do if the 'Japs' invaded. Even 65 years on, his face hardens as he relives the fears of that uncertain time. 'The first one down the hallway was going to get his head blown off, that's for sure,' he says.

He did well at work, making anti-aircraft guns, but he was on 'starvation' apprentice wages – a sixth of a tradesman's wage – and dabbled in minor crime to raise spending money. To his joy, his mother returned safely in 1943 with an inheritance from the death of her father the old Naval officer. She bought a house in Essendon and the family was reunited. But by this time her Billy had a bad name with the local police and there was nothing she could do.

When he turned 18, he tried to enlist in the local drill hall but was refused because his work making guns was vital to the war effort. As more of his dance hall and work mates joined up, he tried twice more.

After the third attempt, his boss called him away from his lathe and into his office at the ordnance factory and read the riot act. He warned him that even if he managed to bluff his way into the services and onto a troopship, he would be sent back from the Middle East because his job was worth 'three or four soldiers'.

He often wondered, later, how his life would have turned out had he got into the army. He fancies that war might have suited him more than most. If there was one thing that stood out about him later, he was cool under fire.

As it was, he worked hard all week but was a weekend tearaway who waged a private war with the local police after making the mistake of beating one constable in a street fight. The inevitable payback for this unpardonable offence was to be thrown in the cells and beaten up by several police, obliged to back up their colleague.

Those were the rules on the streets of Ascot Vale in the 1940s. It was to have lasting effects. When the war ended and the munitions factory wound down, Longley was a skilled tradesman. He still has his set of framed indentures and is proud of them. But he claims he lost three engineering jobs in quick succession because police warned employers against him. So he retreated into the 'knockabout' world. He spent six months working in a rabbit-skinning works then moved up to a job on the wharves. By then he was carrying a pistol. He had been a street fighter – 'all in, no boxing' – since he was at primary school. One afternoon in his late teens, he says, 'I had the good luck to run against three blokes and get over the top (defeat) of all of them. That night I went to the pictures, and I saw one of them. He looked at me and pulled back his jacket so I could see what he had stuck in his belt.' It was a pistol. There was a lot of Colt .45s around because American servicemen on leave had a habit of losing or selling them.

That moment in the cinema was, he says, when he realised that 'the stoush was dead and good street fighters were tuppence a ton'. He walked through the darkened cinema to the emergency exit, unbolted the door and went home. By the following Saturday night he had a pistol, too. And the beginning of a reputation that could have destroyed him.

Longley is living back in the streets of Ascot Vale where he grew up, within walking distance of the showgrounds where, as a boy, he climbed grandstands at night and caught roosting pigeons to sell to Chinese restaurants. 'Amazing how many pigeons you can fit into your shirt,' he muses.

He is sitting in the living room of the tired cream brick unit he rents. Can't keep a dog because the yard is too small, he says. He loves dogs. One of his favourite books in jail – besides the British commando fitness manual – was about the history and breeding of the English bull mastiff.

Longley had a favourite bull mastiff once, when he lived in Port Melbourne with his then young daughter Lisa and her mother. He says the dog was intelligent and alert and probably saved his life during the dock war.

'The dog kept looking up at the roof as he walked around the back yard. He knew something was wrong. I said to my wife "pack a bag – we're going away for a few days".' The Longleys stayed in a friend's house on the NSW south coast. While they were gone, a next-door neighbour – coincidentally called Bill – had a frightening experience. As he was going through his front gate, his wife called out his name. Immediately, three men with shotguns stood up from behind the parapet on Longley's roof. They were rival painters and dockers, lying in wait for Longley, and had been ready to shoot when they heard the name 'Bill'.

Longley was never without a bull mastiff for years after

that. But now, he says, he can't walk a dog enough, though the exercise bike in the hall is helping him get a little fitter. He has always needed exercise to keep his weight down. He has a weakness for strong tea and chocolates.

Family photographs line the walls of his flat and the bookcase is crammed with histories, biographies, dictionaries and a thesaurus. His favourite is Australian correspondent Chester Wilmot's acclaimed war history *The Struggle For Europe*. 'Billy was always the best-read gunman on the docks,' says an erudite friend.

He goes into town to watch a film now and again with his friend and carer, Frances, who lives next door. His favourite film is *On The Waterfront*. Always methodical, he knows what he wants to see next. At the time of writing it was *Downfall*, the European film about Hitler's last days. 'It got five stars in *The Age*,' he says. And television? Twice a week he watches the *The Bill*. Of course. He likes realistic dramas that show flawed characters on both sides of the law.

Longley doesn't rate himself a punter. But he admits he once lost 8000 pounds – then the price of a big house or several small ones – at Canterbury races in the 1960s. He was flying high at the time but soon came back to earth. He reputedly got a share of Australia's then biggest armed robbery in 1970, when three masked men took $587,890 from an armoured van. Twice he thought he was on the way to being a millionaire, he says, but in the end he found out that his mother was right: Crime didn't pay. He lost the money – and 13 years 'buried' in jail while his only daughter grew up and the world passed him by.

Once, he told his brother Reg he dreamed of flying to England, catching the Concorde supersonic airliner to New York and cruising home on the Queen Mary. He never did get to leave Australia – but, two years later, his brother the suburban barber did his dream trip: Concorde, ocean liner and all. He tells the story against himself. It is his way of obliquely acknowledging that he took the wrong fork in the path.

His trips out of Melbourne in the past were mostly at night, by road. He and unnamed others would drive to Sydney overnight in time to arrive with the morning traffic, 'do our business' and then leave again in the afternoon peak. It was safer that way. If they had flown, the police and certain well-informed Sydney gangsters would have known as soon as they got off the plane. The consequences could have been fatal.

One of his signature sayings is 'Sydney for money, Melbourne for blokes.' Meaning that you could stay out of sight ('in smoke') in Melbourne because loyal people would protect you, but would immediately be sold out in Sydney. In the underworld version of traditional Melbourne-Sydney rivalry, he says, Sydney crime bosses traditionally imported Melbourne hard men to fight their battles when the going got tough.

Now, he lives with his memories – and a lot of regrets. One is the death of his first wife in a shooting incident of which he was acquitted. Another is that he didn't shoot Jack Twist at Webb Dock back in 1971. Another is that when he was desperate for cash he pawned his grandfather's gold fob watch in the late 1940s. His mother brought it back from Scotland to give to him in 1943 and he would like it more than anything else. It is engraved with his grandfather's name: Lieutenant Commander William Roxburgh.

If anyone out there has it, he'd kill to get it back. Figuratively speaking, of course.

Bill Longley died at Royal Melbourne Hospital on the morning of 27 March 2014.

CHAPTER 4
GIRLS WHO LIKE BAD BOYS

The men live fast and die young or rot in jail. Their women have to cope with the mess that's left behind.

The last time Sylvia saw Nik Radev alive he was standing at the door of their daughter's flat, head cocked, looking at her in a way that didn't match the tough-guy talk. It was probably as close to wistful as a sociopath gunman and drug dealer ever gets.

'You don't look happy,' she had said to him – sympathetically, she thought later, considering how cruelly he'd treated her for years.

'I'm all right, love,' he said. 'But I got a $100,000 contract on my head.'

Why not go overseas, she asked, then added sardonically: 'Oh yeah, I forgot: you gotta make a million dollars first.'

The way she remembers it, a flash of his old gangster bravado returned. 'I'm not going anywhere,' he snarled at her. 'No-one will touch me.'

But before he went he stepped forward and kissed her softly on the forehead. It was the most tender gesture he'd made towards her in 20 years. She knew then that it meant goodbye.

Two weeks later Nik 'The Bulgarian' Radev was extremely dead – shot seven times in a Coburg street, yet another scene in the ongoing underworld war that looked as if it could have been directed by Quentin Tarantino. Except, of course, that the blood and the bullets were real. It took a team of undertakers to tidy up the corpse before they put it in the gold-lined casket paid for with the fat wads of drug money that had also paid for Radev's $55,000 dental crowns, his Mercedes sports car and an opulent lifestyle that had no legal means of support.

The hitman thought to have killed Radev (and several others), Andrew 'Benji' Veniamin, was himself shot a year later in a restaurant by well-known Carlton identity Dominic 'Mick' Gatto, who is awaiting trial on murder charges at the time of writing.

Sylvia Radev didn't go to the funeral. She had never liked the gangsters her husband had run with and now, at 39, she was free of them at last.

A hail of bullets had done what Hail Marys and divorce papers could not. She felt sorry for their daughter at losing her father – but for herself, she mostly felt relief. She thought she could finally get on with the life Radev had hijacked when she was 17.

But it's not that easy to put the pieces back together, patch up fractured family ties and lead a normal life when people stare and whisper and call you a gangster's moll.

This is how it goes for those who find themselves married to the mob. The men live fast and die young or rot in jail. Their women have to cope with the mess that's left behind.

In a few short months Roberta Williams went from being an unknown nobody to the best-known nobody in town. She of the toothy smile, pugnacious attitude and sharp tongue – and that slightly incongruous name – is a staple in the media coverage of Melbourne's underworld shootings and their aftermath.

Roberta has shot to fleeting fame with the gangland killings – about which she knows nothing, of course, except that her chubby hubby Carl Williams didn't do it. Carl, who had a baby face and a lot of dead acquaintances, was in custody pending trial on several charges at the time of writing. A judge and jury ultimately decided he would stay behind bars but a badly-chosen cell-mate would end it all for him with an iron bar taken from a prison exercise bike.

Meanwhile, Roberta does the talking in the Williams family. There she is, on the court steps, standing by her man. Here she is, grieving for Carl's slain bodyguard, the terminally-tattooed Andrew 'Benji' Veniamin, her 'best friend' and one of several gunmen she has known too well. Now she's holding court at the 'christening' of her daughter at Crown Casino. She scuffles with a cop as the cameras roll and hi-jacks attention at her former father-in-law's funeral by 'clipping' a younger and much blonder woman who had been a rival for Carl's wandering attention.

Roberta always fancied being the centre of attention and the idea of easy money, according to those who have watched her progress. It's just that she somehow managed to scramble onto a bigger stage than she was used to, rubbing against hard men with cash and guns in their pockets. As teenagers, Roberta and her sister were well known to police in Melbourne's distant bayside suburbs. Police around Frankston and Seaford grew tired of removing Roberta from nightclubs and dances where she was guaranteed to make a scene.

She is proof, says one ex-policeman who is now a respected private eye, that 'you can take the girl out of Frankston but can't take Frankston out of the girl.'

Not that she sees herself that way, of course. Roberta has often said she and Carl and the kids were a normal family minding their own business, whatever that was. The truth is, she is starring in her own grubby soap opera and loving it, while the rest of the community – the ones the underworld calls 'squareheads' – look on in bemused fascination, like rubbernecks at a car crash.

So what is it with women and crooks?

Legitimate people, Damon Runyon wrote in the 1930s, 'are much interested in the doings of tough guys, and consider them very romantic.' The heady mix of predatory worthlessness, reckless courage and apparent offhand generosity has always attracted people. Some women find it irresistible, even in villains that others shy away from. In Runyon's terms, where you've got tough guys, you've got dolls.

There's a little bit of Runyon's Broadway in Melbourne, not to mention Al Capone's Chicago. Although the spotlight has paused on Roberta Williams repeatedly, she is just one of a chorus line of gangsters' women. A co-star in the same grisly drama is the tragic Judy Moran, the gangster gran whose blonde mane and heaving bosom have stood out in a sea of black at the funerals of her two sons – Jason and Mark Moran – and two husbands, Les 'Johnny' Cole and Lewis Moran.

Now here's a woman who has suffered terribly for her dubious taste in men. Yet even after the heartbreak of losing both sons, she orchestrated the murder of her brother-in-law Des 'Tuppence' Moran, a crime that will probably see her die in jail.

It's clear that crooks pull women. The question is: why? It's obvious that this often fatal attraction is not logical – but it might well be biological.

Roberta Williams and Judy Moran wouldn't know Lady Macbeth from a Big Mac, but a Melbourne psychologist – and former homicide detective, aptly enough – says that both of them remind him of what he calls the 'Lady Macbeth' stereotype.

Alex Bartsch, who became a psychologist after leaving the police force in the mid-1990s, says there are three other recognisable types – 'risk-takers', 'Florence Nightingales' and 'helpless dependents' – all of whom can be found waiting to see their men on prison visiting days.

'Criminals' wives can be pretty much like celebrities' wives,' Bartsch says. 'They fall into definable types with different motives.' He explains that Lady Macbeth types ruthlessly chase power and influence, no matter what it takes. Then there are those attracted by risk-taking, the whiff of danger, the 'glamour' and the notion they are being 'individual' and 'interesting' by hanging out with lawbreakers. 'Danger and risk-taking have always been aphrodisiacs,' Bartsch says, pointing to a phenomenon that is noticeable in wartime, when shared danger heightens fatalism and breaks down the conventions and inhibitions of peacetime.

The 'Florence Nightingales' are more altruistic than the risk-takers. They are the little girls who nurse wounded birds and stray kittens then graduate to attempting to rescue wounded men when they grow up. Some of them like the idea of a being in emotional control of a man – 'the caged beast' – who pines for them in prison in a romantic way that usually dissolves when he gets out of jail. There is an element of one-upmanship and competitiveness, as with owners of large and dangerous dogs who secretly like the fact that other people are afraid of the beast they imagine is under their control. The difference being that savage dogs are less likely to turn on their owners than gangsters are to turn on their women.

Finally, there are the 'doormats', helpless dependents often found in ethnic crime groups where marriage within the group (or even the extended family) is common, and traditional gender roles are not questioned. This group, brilliantly portrayed in the television crime series The Sopranos, cook and clean and bear children and don't ask questions of their man as long as he provides well for the family.

'Their entire sense of worth is tied to having a relationship – any relationship,' says Bartsch. And, of course, trading sex and obedience for the financial security and precarious prestige of being married to a gangster appeals to some women more than having to make their own way in the world. In every stratum of society and every ethnic group there are those men with power, influence and money whose source of income is politely overlooked by poorer people with daughters of marriageable age. It is the human condition.

'I was a little Italian virgin – innocent and gullible,' Sylvia Radev says with a sigh, nodding at the framed photograph of her teenage self: a touchingly pretty girl headed for heartbreak.

She giggles, still girlish for a 40-year-old who has had a hard life. 'I'd never even seen a penis when I met Nik – let alone one with a tattoo on it,' she says. 'He had "TAXI" on his – because it "went everywhere", he told me.' She parodies her former husband's eastern European accent, giving it a sinister twist. No wonder. Even among bad men, Nik Radev's wicked ways raised eyebrows.

He once held a gun to Sylvia's head as she held their infant daughter. Another time he wanted to prostitute her and told her that the only reason he married her was to get an Australian passport.

How a respectable convent girl ended up with such a monster is a cautionary tale. She begins it with a plea not to reveal her family name in print. Her parents and two older sisters are ashamed – and still frightened – to be linked to Radev, and Sylvia worries that her respectable neighbours will hold it against her if they find out who she was married to. The man's malign influence reaches even from the grave.

At the time of writing, Sylvia was living in a modern brick veneer in Melbourne's south-eastern suburban sprawl. In a small, neat house with a small, neat Japanese car in the driveway, as comfortingly anonymous as thousands of others in any outer suburb in Australia. A huge picture of a tiger hangs over the couch and prints of zebras and other big game animals are on the walls. The furniture is stained pine, faux colonial. It's painstakingly tidy, but warm and welcoming.

Wearing tight jeans and with her ash blonde hair cut short, Sylvia looked and sounded younger than her 40 years. People sometimes mistake her and her then 22-year-old daughter, Raquel, for sisters.

Raquel was painfully thin, with troubled eyes above the high cheekbones she inherited from her father, who used to boast to her that he was descended from Genghis Khan's Tartar warriors that once invaded the part of eastern Europe he came from.

Of Raquel, her mother says: 'She's seen too many bad things.' On the day Sylvia Radev was interviewed by the author, Raquel arrived in a taxi and 'borrowed' $26 from her mother for the fare. Sylvia gave her the cash but reddened with suppressed anger because it was almost all the money she had in her purse. It made an incongruous scene, given that she had been married to a gangster who once threw cash around like confetti. Later, she shows off a decorative screen she restored after salvaging it from a rubbish skip.

After moving 'maybe 30 times' in 22 years, Sylvia says she craves stability. She says she never wants gangsters or police in her home again. She talks about drug squad raids in which, she says, personal possessions mysteriously went missing. In her previous life, before Nik Radev's sudden death, police once found a pistol taped under a cabinet in Raquel's bedroom in a house in the upmarket Melbourne bayside suburb of Brighton. Radev had hidden it, but forced his daughter to lie that another criminal, by then conveniently dead, had put the gun there.

Sylvia says she is determined that her two kindergarten age children (to her new partner) will not be exposed to the things that have made Raquel such a troubled young woman. She doesn't swear or smoke in front of them and spells out words ('K-I-L-L' and 'G-U-N') she thinks unsuitable for the tender ears of those of tender years.

The way she tells it, life is not easy. Sylvia's parents migrated from Calabria in the 1950s. Her father was a driving instructor who paid off a two-storey house in Melbourne's outer eastern suburbs. Her sisters married young and have led law-abiding lives. Which is how Sylvia's life seemed destined to unfold, too, if Nikolai Radev hadn't trapped her.

She left school early to do a hairdressing apprenticeship. At 17 she was working with a Bulgarian woman she won't name – but who, she says, was an activist involved in bringing Bulgarian 'refugees' to Australia.

She says the Bulgarian woman called her a 'rich Italian virgin nun', a reference to her virginity and her hardworking parents' comparative affluence. One day, the woman read tarot cards to her, predicting she would marry a man from 'far away'. Sylvia was fascinated. Later, she was to see the fortune-telling episode as part of a web that snared her.

Soon after the tarot card reading, two young Bulgarians turned up at the salon. They spoke poor English, but one spoke Italian. They were new arrivals being helped by Sylvia's boss.

After the pair left, the woman asked Sylvia which one of them she liked.

Neither, she said. But if you had to choose, the woman pressed, which one? Sylvia shrugged. The sporty-looking one, she said, meaning the one who spoke Italian and was 'well dressed'. What she meant was that he had worn white tracksuit and runners and looked athletic.

What she didn't know was that under the tracksuit, as well as his fit wrestler's physique, were 'jail tatts', legacy of a shadowy past in Europe. At 22, young Nikolai Radev had already served time in Europe. Far from being a genuine refugee, she later found out, he was a black marketer and probably an army deserter who had gamed the system to get to Australia after being refused entry to the United States. He needed to marry an Australian citizen to get a passport and permanent residency. A street-smart operator whose own peasant background allowed him to understand conservative religious migrant groups, he instinctively knew that his best chance of arranging a suitable marriage quickly was to target traditional people like Sylvia's parents.

For Sylvia herself, such insights into Radev's motives lay in the future. Back in 1980, all she knew was that the 'sporty one', Nikolai the wrestler, kept turning up. The first time he brought her violets – not a bunch of flowers, but the whole plant in a pot. It seemed quirky and sweet. She didn't know that he had probably stolen it from someone's porch just before he presented it to her.

Radev manipulated her. It wasn't hard. She was 17 and as green as grass. It helped, of course, that Sylvia didn't fancy the 'nice' Italian boy her parents had wanted her to marry. She wanted to escape her family's strict control – and marriage to someone other than the arranged suitor seemed one way out. When the Bulgarian woman arranged for them all to meet at a social function, Radev charmed Sylvia's parents, speaking Italian to them and making a great show of listening attentively to what they had to say. They were easy meat for an accomplished con man, one who had worked his way from the backblocks of Bulgaria through Europe to a new country.

Naturally, according to the strict Catholic culture of Sylvia's parents, courtship soon led to an engagement. That way Nik was sometimes allowed to see her without some sort of chaperone. He understood this and so was able to soothe her parents' feelings. One day he got permission to take her for an apparently innocent outing. Instead, he took her to a motel room in St Kilda. It is hard to believe it was the surprise that she later suggested it was. She was, after all, 17 and believed herself 'in love'. But, for the cold-blooded Radev, setting her up was simply a way of closing the deal that would guarantee him a passport and residency.

'I thought it would be like the Rod Stewart song *Tonight's The Night* – all romantic,' Sylvia recalls, grimacing at her naiveté. 'It wasn't. He virtually raped me. He broke me and hurt me. Then he said: "Now you'll have to marry me. No-one else will have you".'

It was the beginning of her education. She started to see a calculating criminal mind in everything her husband-to-be did. He even used red wax salvaged from a cheese rind to forge a seal on a phony baptism certificate so that they could be married at St Anthony's Church in Hawthorn.

They spent their wedding night at a big Melbourne hotel. Next morning, her parents came to take them to the airport for a honeymoon in Tasmania. Before they left the hotel, the cunning Radev deliberately cut himself, put blood on the sheets and showed it to them: 'proof' that their daughter had been a virgin.

The honeymoon was at the then fashionable Wrest Point Casino in Hobart. The way Sylvia recalls it, her new husband gambled while she stayed in their room. Within a few days he forced her to persuade her parents to send more money because he had blown all their wedding present cash.

Sylvia fell pregnant. At five months, she was hurt in a road smash when Radev drove his car in front of another car so that it hit the passenger side. She lost the baby, a boy, but Radev didn't come to the hospital and didn't call her mother for many hours. Later, she wondered if he had been trying to kill her. Even then, the strongest feeling she had for him was fear, even after her daughter Raquel was born in 1982.

Apart from a few months in a pizza shop and a few more in a glass factory, Nik didn't work. Sylvia, still hairdressing, borrowed to buy a house in Hampton Park. But a year later Nik was charged with armed robbery and demanded she sign papers to sell the house: he wanted the money to flee the country before the trial.

She didn't want to sell but he didn't want to know. 'He held a gun to my head while I was holding the baby and said if I didn't sign he would kill me,' she was to recall. 'It traumatised Raquel because I was terrified and holding her so tight. I signed, but I was crying so much I left drips on the paper.'

The house was sold but Radev's audacious escape plan went wrong. When they got to the airport, his name was flagged on the passport alert system and the police grabbed him. He went to jail.

Sylvia filed for divorce. But that didn't matter to Radev. When he got out, he turned up when it suited him – a pattern he was to repeat for years. Sylvia eventually found another partner but Radev bashed him, breaking his teeth, and threatened 'to put him in the boot' – a reference to putting his rival's body in the boot of a car.

Sylvia was frightened that he meant it. She would put nothing past him. Whenever he was out of jail, it was understood that her new partner – a quiet 'squarehead' who works in a factory – would make himself scarce if Radev came around to see her and Raquel.

When Raquel was nine years old, Radev took mother and daughter to Bulgaria so his parents could see their grandchild. On the first night in Europe, in a hotel room in Germany, he frightened Sylvia by toying with a hairdryer and joking about electrocuting her as she took a bath. She took showers from then on.

In his hometown in Bulgaria, Radev pointed out a third storey balcony to Sylvia. Then he told her with great relish that when he was eight years old, he had pushed an old man off the balcony 'just to see what it was like to see someone die.'

She realised then that he was either a psychopathic killer or a psychopathic liar. Either way, it didn't make for a restful holiday. Neither did his 'jokes' about killing her 'for the insurance'. Something about Radev's 'sense of humour' unnerved her.

Oddly enough, she liked his family and they liked her. Sylvia and little Raquel enjoyed visiting the Radev family farm, where the old people ploughed their land with horses, tended their own pigs, poultry and sheep and grew most of their own food. They seemed to like her, too, and were apologetic about their renegade son – and grateful that he had found such a nice wife.

But she was never to forget that Nik's brother, Stoyan, once said to her in private in his broken English: 'Sorry,

Sylvie, sorry. Nikolai is no good.' It was good advice, but too late.

Sylvia was keen to leave Bulgaria and travel to her family's home town in Calabria, where her father's brothers still lived. There, she was confident that Radev would not do anything to harm her. He knew better than to upset Calabrians in family matters and so she felt safe there.

In Europe, they travelled as man and wife but back in Australia, life resumed its strange pattern, with Radev coming and going whenever Sylvia took his fancy. She knew he had other women — often drug-addicted prostitutes or lap dancers – and he even fathered children with them. 'Junkies got involved with him and had children – it was tragic.' But she felt powerless to do anything about it.

'I served the divorce papers on him when he was in jail when Raquel was three. He didn't like that and when he got out he came in and out of my life. The cycle kept repeating itself. My relatives said 'get away from him' but I couldn't. I was scared he would find me.

'He was so intimidating, you just let him do it. Just shut up and let him,' she told the author. 'Some girls are gangsters' molls – they love being in that environment. But I don't. I didn't like the vibes and didn't like the people he brought with him. I don't trust them.'

She recalls meeting the established 'number one mistress' of a well-known standover man and racketeer prominent in the Italian-dominated 'Carlton crew'. The woman, a hairdresser with her own salon, had two children to the gangster which were later sent to prominent private schools. The friendship between the two women wasn't encouraged: the Italian heavyweight didn't want Radev's woman knowing too much about his private affairs. It could make him vulnerable to the scheming Bulgarian.

Sylvia had other insights into her ex-husband's murky world. 'I met a guy called Ange who lived in hotels to stay away from people who might want to find him. These Greek girls like him. He would give them money for plastic surgery and dangle drugs in front of them.'

But Sylvia knew that drug money was fool's gold because it came at too great a price – other people's ruined lives and loss of her own self-respect, legacy of her strict upbringing. She knew that her parents and her sisters and their husbands were afraid of Radev. Her parents fortified their house with heavy doors so that it would be difficult to break into. They feared Radev's activities could make them a target.

'I used to say to myself: "When is he (Radev) going to drop dead? He doesn't deserve to be alive".'

When it finally happened, she was shocked but hardly surprised.

It was much worse for her daughter, Raquel. Despite all her father had put her through, she still loved him. And the timing was bad: he had been about to pay $20,000 for her to undergo a revolutionary drug detoxification treatment in Israel when he was killed.

Nothing in Sylvia or Raquel's modest circumstances suggests they got anything but grief from Radev's life of crime and violent death. Some of his associates did, Sylvia says. But it didn't last long. His 'driver' Mark Mallia was murdered not long afterwards.

They buried Nik Radev in a gold-plated casket worth $30,000, carried by menacing men in black. But when Sylvia took their daughter to find his grave several months later, there was no headstone, and the plot was covered in weeds. There was little for them to remember but painful memories. Sylvia put a packet of his favourite Dunhill cigarettes on the grave and left. She hasn't been back since.

Maria Arena was in the kitchen with her younger son when she heard the shot that ended 25 years of marriage. By the time they reached her Joe he was dead, shot from behind as he put out the garbage bin.

It was midnight. The Arenas had just got home to Bayswater, an outer suburb in the foothills of the

Dandenongs east of Melbourne, after a wedding in Footscray, on the other side of the city. There was a big chance the killer had known where they'd been, knew when their Toyota would pull into the drive. That probability is something Joe Arena's family don't want to think about, let alone talk about.

But the awful truth is that the 'hit' must have been an inside job. A year before there had been another big Italian wedding, when the Arenas' daughter Lisa had got married. Almost certainly, among the 450 guests at the lavish reception in Brunswick was someone who was simultaneously enjoying Joe Arena's hospitality – and plotting his execution. That thought still gnaws at Maria Arena.

Of all the wedding guests, those who ate and drank and kissed the proud parents, only a few comforted the stricken widow and children after Joe's funeral. The rest, she said bitterly at the time, 'dropped off like flies', as if the whole family had been buried with him. If that is the Calabrian way, she said then, she wanted no part of it.

That was in 1988. For six years, Maria stayed in the family house, sleeping just a few metres from where Joe had been gunned down, nursing grief and anger that she later admitted kept some people away. In 1994 she finally sold up and moved to a small unit a few streets away.

Time has dulled her anger but it hasn't solved her husband's murder. Police believe they know how and why the plot unfolded. They say that Giuseppe 'Joe' Arena was tied to the Calabrian crime group, the Honoured Society. As an insurance broker and financial adviser, they say, he helped launder cash for marijuana growers in Griffith and Mildura.

Maria concedes that Joe was worried for weeks before he died. Police believe he borrowed a pistol, though he gave it back to the lender before he was killed. And whereas he would normally drink at social functions ('We would be first there, last to leave,' says Maria) and she would drive, on the last night of his life he drank nothing and drove home himself. 'Maybe he heard something,' Maria says, 'but he thought it would sort itself out.'

Police say Arena's reputation as a shrewd financial head had led the secret society's Godfather, Liberio Benvenuto, to anoint him as his successor. But, after Benvenuto's death in June 1987, ruthless rivals jostling for power in the Honoured Society decided to kill Arena and take over. Police think Arena, only 50, sold up his moderate business interests after Benvenuto's death as if he expected a fresh source of income.

But his widow disputes the theory that he was setting up as the new Godfather. 'He might have known these people (the Honoured Society) but it was only through business clients,' she insists.

Nothing about Maria Arena or the way she lives hints that her husband was anything other than she claims: a hard-working family man who had climbed from poverty to pay off a house, a car and some investments. 'We were comfortable but a lot of our friends had bigger houses than we did,' she says. 'When the fraud squad checked everything after he died they said we had a nice little house but it wasn't a marijuana palace.'

Certainly, Maria seems an ordinary suburban grandmother. She opens the door of her unassuming unit wearing a striped pinafore over sensible slacks and blouse. She looks as if she has been baking cakes in case the grandkids visit, which is exactly what she does do.

A gangster's wife? It seems ridiculous. She doesn't fit any stereotypes. Not the faded glamour girl with the big hair, the winter tan, plastic surgery and loud jewellery. Nor the traditional Italian widow in black. She looks like a middle-aged department store assistant – which she is, up the road at Knox City shopping centre. She loves her job because she likes talking to people.

Maria Arena is short, in her late 50s, with golden brown eyes, rosy cheeks and fair skin. Her mother's family was from Subiaco, near Rome, and her father was Yugoslav, so she is not tied by blood or custom to the tight knit Calabrian clans she married into. Having arrived in Australia at five years old, she speaks English as if born here. Her children have Anglo names. None of them now has much to do with the Calabrian community.

The way she tells it, her marriage was just another modest migrant success story – apart from the ending. It started when she was 17 and began work for an Italian-run concreting firm at Lilydale that needed an office girl fluent in both English and Italian. Joe, eight years older, was her boss's cousin. He worked at a nearby cafe where she went for coffee, and nature took its course. Within a year, she was engaged, pregnant and married, in that order. They were to have three children in four years.

They opened a dress shop but it failed. 'Joe worked three jobs to pay off the debts so he wouldn't be known as a bankrupt,' Maria says. He worked shifts in a factory, mowed lawns and started selling insurance and real estate on the side. They tried a fruit shop but Joe was so good with insurance and real estate that he took it on full time.

'He had the gift of the gab and he was likeable,' she says. 'He always had time for old people and they trusted him.' Trust was vital: many older migrants spoke little English and were illiterate. They trusted Arena to handle their affairs and he became an influential figure in the Italian community.

Maria fetches a framed snap of Joe. It shows a dark, nattily-dressed man with the signature smile that led the media to dub him 'the friendly Godfather'.

He was so gentle, she says, that the only time he spanked their younger son – for setting fire to the garage – 'he felt so sick about it he went to bed' instead of going to work.

She tells other stories. Once, a jealous workmate at the National Mutual insurance company tried to undermine him by complaining about his spelling. The workmate received a memo from the boss saying, 'If you were as good at your job as Joe Arena is at his, you wouldn't have to worry about spelling.' The rest of the memo was deliberately misspelt to make a point. Maria loves telling that story.

Jealousy is a recurring theme. Maria refuses to speculate about who ordered Joe's murder but she suggests he was too popular for his own good – that maybe others thought he was currying favour with certain people.

But he did not just inspire jealousy – he could be extremely jealous himself. Asked if he had ever been in trouble, Maria gets tears in her eyes. 'We had a bad patch in our marriage once,' she quavers. It is the only reference she makes to the fact Joe was convicted of manslaughter in 1976 for killing a man he thought was her lover. He served just two years jail for his crime of passion.

He was, she says, an intelligent man whose life was governed by his lack of education. Had he been educated 'he could have been a lawyer or some other profession.' She means he would also still be alive.

Maria says she is not rich. She lives on her small wage and rent from an investment property. Joe's superannuation is invested to leave to her children. Her greatest pleasure now is to be 'Nonna' to her grandchildren.

The youngest grandson was only four when she spoke to the author. The little boy is bold and cheerful and reminds her of the grandfather he will never know. 'Sometimes I look in his eyes and say "Are you in there, Joe Arena?"'

And her eyes are bright with tears again.

When Sandra met Sammy he had been tried for murder and convicted of armed-robbery and escape and was serving 18 years. He was 42 with a face, as one jail mate joked, 'like five miles of bad road.'

Sandra was 23, attractive, with three small daughters and the chance to improve on the violent alcoholic husband she had left behind in Canberra. The daughter of poor but respectable enough migrants – her father was Spanish-born, her mother English – she had arrived from Coventry in Britain as an eight-year-old and started life in the new country in Nissen huts at the Maribyrnong migrant hostel. Hers was a big family of battlers who did the best they could.

Why she would volunteer to visit a prisoner, let alone one with Sam Hutchinson's record, is hard to know. He himself was surprised – and tried to discourage her.

'I got a letter from her and I ignored it,' he recalls. He saw no point in forming a friendship under the circumstances – he was doing a long sentence for armed robberies – 'but after a few weeks I gave in.' As it turned out, the surprise visit was the result of some sly matchmaking by one of Sandra's brothers, who was serving time with Hutchinson following involvement in a street fight that had turned ugly. Sandra's brother told her that Sam was 35, not 42, and that his sense of humour made up for his hard looks. She says she just wanted someone to visit.

That was in early 1981. Now, against all odds, Sam and Sandra Hutchinson are not only married but still together and going well. The prison system throws up some unlikely love stories but few jail romances last on the outside the way theirs has.

Hutchinson has been home with Sandra since he was paroled in 1991 and hasn't been in any trouble. She has held the same job for 15 years and has almost paid off their house in an outer western suburb. He stays home and does the housework.

At 66, Hutchinson still looks like an artist's impression of a cartoon villain – broken nose, stubble, close-cropped hair, barrel chest. He talks fast and laughs a lot but there is no mistaking why he was once the barber of Pentridge's notorious H Division, a job reserved for hard men. Sandra, by contrast, looks as if butter wouldn't melt in her mouth. When the author calls she is wearing an expensive woollen sweater, well-cut slacks and elegant leather shoes – an outfit that wouldn't look out of place with a Volvo and a golden retriever in the middle-class suburbs of any Australian city.

It looks a simple case of the 'Florence Nightingale' syndrome, where a strong woman saves a flawed man. But it's more complicated than that, as real life usually is. In fact, this polite and pleasant woman played Bonnie to her man's Clyde for nine weeks on the run.

It was late 1982, a few months after they married in Sale Prison, where Hutchinson had been sent from Pentridge. Sandra was living with her children in a flat in St Albans in Melbourne's west, and regularly travelled to Sale by train to visit him. She knew he was getting restless. He sent her a cryptic letter, saying he was waiting for 'a space ship to land'. Sandra read him loud and clear. She left her children at her sister's, hired an old car, drove to Sale and booked into a local motel.

'I didn't sleep at all that night. I knew a million things could go wrong,' she recalls.

Hutchinson, well liked by prison governors and warders because of his knockabout humour and fighting ability, was trusted to work on prison gardens outside the wall. Next morning, minutes after he walked out the front gate, Sandra pulled up in the deserted street next to the old red brick prison and he jumped in the car. By the time the road blocks went up they were in Melbourne. They spent the first night of their 'honeymoon' in a caravan park on the Ballarat Road in the distinctly unromantic outer suburb of Deer Park.

Next day, with Sandra's children still staying at her sister's, they went driving. Near Frankston, a traffic policeman on a motorcycle saw Sandra drive through an amber light but when he pulled them over he didn't recognise her polite passenger as the prison escapee whose picture was in every newspaper that morning. When the policeman asked Sandra what she was doing so far from St Albans, she replied pertly: 'My husband hasn't had a holiday for years and I'm taking him for one.' He fined her for going through the light. She made sure she paid the fine next day. There was no need to tempt fate any more than necessary.

They were broke. Hutchinson knew only one way to get money – armed robbery. He prevailed on his impressionable young bride to buy a shotgun advertised in a newspaper – which was then legal – and then he sawed off the barrels to make it easy to hide. They moved from the caravan park to a Carlton boarding house.

'We booked in under the name "Floyd" – as in "Pretty Boy Floyd",' recalls Hutchinson.

While they were there the boarding house was surrounded and raided by people they assumed were plainclothes police. Luckily, Hutchinson didn't reach for the shotgun he had stashed under the couch. It turned out that it wasn't police but federal agents chasing illegal immigrants. The agents never knew that they had spoken to one of Australia's most wanted men – and that he had a sawn-off shotgun in the room.

While they were in the boarding house, they heard sirens and saw police cars in the street outside. At first, they thought that this time it had to be the police coming for them. But when the sirens and cars went past, they realised something else must have happened. Then they heard the news – the well-known painter and docker and standover man Brian Kane had been shot dead in the Quarry Hotel just up the road in Brunswick.

Hutchinson was planning to 'knock off' a bank at the corner of Rathdowne and Fenwick Street but decided Carlton was 'too hot'.

'We got too cocky, too confident,' he says. 'I went into a barber's for a haircut and a guy was looking at a picture of me in the newspaper and then looking at me. I'm sure he recognised me but he didn't say anything.'

They bolted from Carlton and went to a flat in St Kilda. Hutchinson robbed several service stations to finance their doomed escapade.

The police caught them two months later, the day they were moving into a rented house with Sandra's children. It ended, mercifully, without Hutchinson shooting anyone but not before he was made number nine on the top ten most wanted men. And so Sandra's dream of domestic bliss went on hold for a decade.

Sam was sentenced to an extra 16 years; Sandra was given a bond for aiding and abetting escape. When he was transferred to country prisons she moved from town to town to make it easier to visit him. The prison officers admired her devotion and gave her coffee and bought lollies for her girls, who called Sam 'Dad'.

'They wondered why a good sort like her was travelling up on the train to visit a deadhead like me, Dangerous Dan McGrew!' chortles the old armed robber and street-fighting man. He is a good talker and a compulsive joker, and can't resist making outrageous wisecracks when Sandra is talking. After all these years, he still makes her laugh.

But it hasn't been all guns and roses. In 1989, they broke up for several months while Sandra and the girls were living in a Latrobe Valley town. It was so serious that Sam, sad but philosophical, gave his wedding ring to a cell mate. Fortunately, the cell mate took the long view and kept the ring safe – and gave it back when Sandra turned up at the prison for a visit several months later and apologised for the split.

Now the girls are grown up with children of their own but they still call him 'Dad'. While Sandra works at a well-known printing works for a national media company, her retired robber restores antique lamps, does the cooking and cleaning and frightens would-be burglars, who reputedly give their street a wide berth. One of his favourite neighbours is an old Calabrian woman who matches his stories with ones about her father, who was an armed bandit in the hills of his native country.

The Hutchinson house is dotted with his antique lamps and a handsome vintage typewriter sits on a side table. The bookshelves are lined with a video library of films and sets of encyclopaedia and reference books.

People from his past sometimes call looking for 'help' but Sandra heads them off. 'I earn enough money to get by so Sam doesn't need to do anything wrong,' she says firmly.

'She's got to be admired for her endeavour,' he says with a grin. 'It's good being a squarehead.'

But they can't help a whiff of nostalgia. When the old Pentridge prison was opened to visitors before being developed as a housing site, they went back for old time's sake.

'You do get a bit sentimental,' muses the serial escaper. 'I looked up at the tower on the wall and I said to Sandra: "You know, I went over that wall twice".'

It seems a good moment to ask a delicate question. Why does he think that some women feel an overwhelming need to form relationships with dangerous men, in and out of jail? Is it a deep-seated instinct to help, or do they just like the excitement?

'Nah,' he says dismissively. 'It's just that crims have big wangers.'

CHAPTER 5
IT'S PAYBACK TIME

They thought they got away with pack raping two 15-year-olds they were sure would stay silent forever. They were wrong.

The leader of the pack is out there, in the suburbs or some country town. He's middle-aged now, probably with a family of his own. If he has teenage daughters, you can bet he's careful where they go and who they're with. He knows bad things can happen – he and his mates used to rape girls that age in the 1970s. It was sport to them, like wild dogs killing sheep.

Maybe he thinks about it sometimes when he's mowing the lawn or washing the car, or when a schoolgirl walks past. Or last thing before he goes to sleep.

No one outside the gang knows exactly how many girls they lured into cars, abducted and violated. There were a lot of gang rapes in the 1970s, and not all were investigated, let alone solved. Often, the victims and their families became part of a conspiracy of silence – gagged by fear, shame and the prospect of blame.

And so the gangs got away with it until something

stopped them: they were caught, or close enough to it to be scared off, or they tired of their brutal game. A few of 'the boys' might have committed other violent crimes and ended up in jail, but the rest faded back into suburban anonymity. Family men with secrets. It would be a lot to presume that many, if any, feel remorse about what they did. But they must wonder in quiet moments whether the past can ever reach out for them.

The answer is that it can. This is the story of how a terrified schoolgirl became a driven and determined adult, hunting a gang of men who raped her when she was 15.

She traced the man who betrayed her by delivering her and her friend to the gang. This time, she guessed, he would betray the same gang. He just didn't know it yet, nor that a detective who worked on the case for ten years had been watching him for weeks.

On the first Tuesday of November, 1976, the rest of the world was watching the United States presidential election: Jimmy Carter versus Gerald Ford in a cliffhanger. But in Australia, the Melbourne Cup pushed the White House off the front page. Even the worst Cup Day weather in memory couldn't stop the race that stops a nation. More than 78,000 turned up at Flemington.

It was a day of portents, humid and oppressive, as if the tropical wet season had strayed south. By early afternoon, thunderclouds blacked out the sun. Anxious drivers turned on headlights even before the first cloudburst hit. Hundreds of cars were stranded in flooded streets. The wind uprooted trees and stripped roofs. Then the rain hit again, turning Flemington into a paddy field of ruined shoes and shattered hopes.

It was the wettest Cup in history. The deluge would stick in people's minds for years. The betting ring was swamped with money for a New Zealand mudlark called Van Der Hum, a dour plodder backed to favouritism who duly splashed his way into racing folklore by winning the slowest Cup in decades.

Hundreds of police were rostered to watch the race crowd. One was Richard Parsons, a 26-year-old constable in uniform, seconded from Footscray. Twenty-six years later, as a veteran detective, he remembered how wet it was and that he found a warm welcome and a few drinks when he finished his shift, at a party hosted by Melbourne socialite Peter Janson in a double-decker bus.

There were other attractions on that public holiday. At Festival Hall in West Melbourne, not far across the industrial sprawl between the docks and the muddy Maribyrnong River, thousands of teenagers queued to get into a concert, Cup Day Rock.

The old boxing stadium was a primitive but popular

venue. Just nine days earlier, some of the biggest Australian acts of the 1970s had packed the hall for the annual Rocktober concert. Now it was full again. The Cup Day concert featured Mark Holden, a clean-cut pop idol who tossed carnations into the crowd and drew adoring teenage girls who'd seen him on the television rock show, *Countdown*. Where girls go, boys follow. Not all of them clean-cut.

The concert ended about 5pm. Ushers opened the back doors into Rosslyn Street to ease the crush around the main doors at the front. The crowd poured into wet streets under a sullen sky.

Among them were two girls, schoolmates who'd caught the train in from the eastern suburbs. They were in third form at high school and had not long started going out by themselves. Donna, curly-haired and vivacious, was dressed in jeans, T-shirt and a blue Lurex cardigan. Angela opted for the hippie look: 'treads' sandals, a long skirt, earrings. They were friends, but not best friends.

Waiting in the street were three youths in a station wagon. Donna had first met two of them at the Rocktober concert nine days before. The shorter, better-looking one she knew as Wayne Thompson. He was fair, with browny-blond hair, cut short in a modified version of the sharpie style. He wore the uniform of the time: a polo shirt with a penguin logo and tight Staggers jeans.

Wayne's mates were both called John. The one Donna had met twice before had pale skin and dark hair with longer 'tails' at the back. The three were in the front bench seat of the fawn-coloured station wagon, probably a Holden, the back packed with tools and building equipment. At 18, they were working men with adult tastes in alcohol, cigarettes and sex.

Donna knew the car. It was the one in which the obliging Wayne had given her a lift to Flinders Street station after the Rocktober concert. The same car that, a few nights later, he had driven all the way from the western suburbs to Box Hill to meet her. She had skipped a ballroom dancing class to meet him and one of the Johns that night – and had agreed to meet them the following Sunday.

That Wayne would drive across town to see her impressed Donna. He was older, had a car and money, and came from somewhere else: among her peers, that made him desirable. She didn't realise it might also make him dangerous.

But there were clues. During the week, a stranger, calling himself 'Tony', telephoned Donna at home asking her to a party.

He said Wayne had given him her number. This

confused her. She wondered why Wayne would hand out her number. She refused.

On the Sunday, she took the train to the city. Wayne met her at Flinders Street station. With him was his supposed 'brother', John, who, Donna later found out, was not related to Wayne at all. This tendency to fudge names puzzled Donna but did not make her suspicious.

They then drove west, across the Dudley flats and the Maribyrnong River and beyond, through suburbs she had never seen. To a deserted picnic area, where there was a public toilet block near a creek, some boulders and scrubby trees. There they met friends of Wayne's, including one called 'Tony'.

It was a trial run, Donna was to realise later. She was naive. She half expected to have sex with Wayne, as she thought of him as her 'boyfriend'. But when he pushed her to 'turn it on' for Tony, she was upset.

Tony forced himself on her and Wayne took photographs, as if she was a trophy. She was angry and humiliated but not scared. She did not yet grasp she was being set up as a target for the gang by being branded a 'slut'.

Which is why, two days later, when Wayne got out of the station wagon outside Festival Hall, she listened to him when he apologised for his behaviour. He said he would make it up to her by taking her and her friend to a party.

At first, Donna played it cool. She said, 'I know what your parties are like,' referring to the Sunday incident. But Wayne was persuasive and plausible. That was why, as she realised much later, it was his job to 'chat up' vulnerable girls picked out of the crowd at concerts. It was the gang's *modus operandi*.

Donna took the bait; she and Angela agreed to go. As soon as he closed the deal, Wayne smoothly switched things: he said that as his car was already full, the girls could get a lift with his friends. He assured them his mates were trustworthy.

On cue, a gleaming red Torana pulled up next to them. It was a two-door manual with black bucket seats, a billiard-ball on the gearstick and a transfer with the word 'Torana' in big white capitals across the top of the windscreen. Four young men were in the car. The driver wore a hat. A big man leaned forward in the passenger seat and unlatched it so Angela could climb in between the pair in the back. Donna realised she was expected to sit on the big man's knee in the front. She was taken aback at first but having to squeeze in seemed so clearly uncomfortable and temporary that it reinforced the impression that the party was nearby.

Wayne assured her he would drive ahead and lead the way. She believed him – and Angela trusted her. It was all organised. In seconds, the situation had changed from the girls going with three people Donna had already met to being in a car full of strangers.

The first thing she realised was that the four men belonged to one ethnic group. They were dark-haired and spoke with the same accent. She thought they were Greek or maybe Italian. In itself, that didn't matter to her. Donna and some of her five siblings were born overseas – to a Canadian father and Northern Irish mother – and the family had been all over the world before immigrating only a few years before, so she knew what it was like to be an outsider.

What made her uneasy was that these strangers knew things about her: which concerts she had been to; that she liked dancing; where she came from and which school she went to.

'They were kind of laughing but in a sly way,' is how she put it later. 'We were being "interviewed" but I didn't know it. They were looking for someone who fitted their criteria: who came from a different area and had no idea who they were or where they were taking us.' The men avoided using each other's names. They called each other 'mate', although she heard the name 'Joe' and one mentioned working in a garage.

What the men knew about her was harmless enough, but

the fact they knew it unsettled her. Donna glanced in the rear-vision mirror and caught the eye of one of the men in the back seat. She didn't like his stare. He was sizing her up.

The longer they drove, the stranger the situation seemed. For the second time in three days, she was driven into the western suburbs. When both cars pulled up at a service station she was uneasy. The one she called the 'big guy' got out and spoke to Wayne secretively. It was as if they were discussing a drug deal.

It was a deal. But not drugs.

The big guy was boss. He was broad-shouldered, thickset and had a strong accent. Donna noticed the distinctive crease across the bridge of his nose.

By the time they left the service station, Donna was spooked but didn't know what to do. Even if she got away, Angela was trapped in the back.

Soon, they left the houses behind and passed open country – the rifle range at Williamstown – then turned off on to a rough dirt track that led into wasteland between the Altona beachfront and a row of huge fuel or chemical storage tanks. In the distance she saw the orange-tiled roofs of a new housing development, but the wasteland was deserted. Thunder rumbled as the cars stopped near a patch of stunted scrub.

Everything was wrong. Donna jumped out of the Torana and ran to Wayne's car, checking over her shoulder that Angela was behind her. 'What's going on?' she yelled at Wayne.

'What's the problem?' he answered, and one of the two with him said something odd: 'We're doing a deal.' An admission.

She heard a thud, a sudden exhalation of air and a scream. She jerked around to see that the big guy had knocked Angela to the ground and was dragging her, like a hunter with an animal carcass. Angela's face was contorted with fear. (Years later, when Donna saw Edvard Munch's painting *The Scream*, it reminded her of the way her friend looked at that moment.)

Donna turned back to Wayne and the two Johns and begged them to do something. One mumbled something about going for help. They got back in their car and drove off.

She never saw them again. It was a set-up.

The big man threw Angela into the Torana. Donna ran at him and jumped on his back, clawing at his neck. He grabbed her and tossed her into the back seat with Angela, who was sobbing. The other two men were still outside, leaving the driver and the leader in the front.

The other two walked off, as if they had rehearsed their

movements. The driver sped off, bouncing over the rough ground, then stopped the car.

Donna was terrified, but she was still thinking. 'You don't want to do this,' she said, but the big guy interrupted.

'Why don't you just fucking shut up,' he said quietly, cold eyes staring into hers. Then she saw the glint of the knife in his hand, held low between the bucket seats.

That's when she knew there was no way out. But she couldn't imagine what was going to happen. How could she? She was 15.

It wasn't until Donna was twice that age, an apparently successful and sophisticated woman living a long way from Melbourne, that she found the words to tell what happened that day.

She had worked hard and lived fast, a party girl running on adrenaline and deadlines, pushing herself to exhaustion so that she could sleep it off and do it all again, night after night. She left school and Melbourne soon after the rapes, started as a window dresser, moved to working in nightclubs and then theatre – steadily more frenetic jobs that kept body and mind busy. It was the mask turned to the world, a way to keep nightmares at bay.

It didn't always work.

Once, in 1983, drunk in an empty club at 5am, she told

a friend she'd been raped, but then fell silent. He did not hear the full story until years later.

After one failed relationship and a few false starts, she stayed single for years. Her family knew what had happened in Melbourne but it was taboo. Her parents had opposed going to the police, moved interstate soon after the ordeal and 'left it behind'. Donna was implicitly encouraged to go along with an unspoken conspiracy to keep it buried for the same reasons many rape victims did and still do: shame, blame and fear. Not only fear of blame and fear of reprisals, but fear of being cross-examined in court and judged outside it.

In any case, for years she could not force herself to talk about it. Until one day in early 1992, when the past finally caught up and her mask cracked.

It happened with a chance sighting at a mailing house where she was approving theatre subscription brochures. A supervisor asked where she went to school, explaining that one of the men working there thought he remembered her face from a high school in Melbourne.

It was a harmless query, but Donna was rattled. Being recognised triggered a rush of submerged memories – and fears. From that day, friends noticed that her behaviour changed.

One of those friends was Tom McDonald, an Australian

business lawyer then practising mostly in the United States but who often visited the city where Donna lived. He first met her in 1991 at the club she then managed. They became friends and he helped her with a legal problem. She repaid him by cooking him dinner when he was in town. To McDonald, Donna was 'sparkling company and a damned good cook' but their friendship was platonic. After one such meal in early 1992, they were listening to music and having a drink when Donna's breezy charm fell apart. She said she trusted him because he had never made a pass at her. Then she said she'd been having 'strange feelings'. Then she broke down.

The savvy club manager turned into a frightened girl. Crying and disjointed, she poured out a stream of raw recollections. 'It was so traumatic it made her physically ill,' McDonald recalls.

Afterwards, he felt 'ashamed to be a man for about five minutes'. Then he decided to help. He suggested psychological treatment – and legal remedies. One avenue was crimes compensation. The other was justice – searching for the attackers and seeing them punished. McDonald helped her launch a crimes compensation case that she eventually won. But mere compensation – about six months' wages for a dozen rapes and a ruined life – was never going to be enough to put her back together again.

In 1992, Donna's friends saw what one calls 'that sparky, mischievous, bossy girl' unravel. The workaholic could no longer work. Her stylish Art Deco inner-suburban house was a mess. She stayed indoors for days, curled in a ball, crying. On her first visit to a psychologist she handed over a tape recording of an interview she had recently had with a sexual assault counsellor. It was, the psychologist said later, 'a harrowing account of a harrowing crime'.

Another friend heard the story first-hand, with detail that shook him – 'all the filthy parts she needed to have said,' he says.

She finally went to the police on 17 March, 1992, while in Melbourne for a conference. She went to Nunawading Community Policing Squad and started talking. It took 10 hours to finish the statement. A kind policewoman took it all down and shared a piece of boiled fruitcake with her, the only thing either of them ate from midday until 10pm.

She recalled every detail as if it were frozen in time. 'I have these snapshots in my brain,' she explained later. 'It unfolds like a film. A noir film.'

It wasn't just the knife but the look in the eyes of the man who held it that terrified Donna. He dragged her out of the car, then got in the back seat and started to rape Angela.

Donna was in shock. The driver stayed in the car,

watching. The other two men walked up. They pushed and abused her, working themselves up. They called her 'fucking slut' and 'stupid bitch' and 'hopeless c...' and grabbed at her breasts. They called her 'boutana' or 'puttana' – Greek and Italian variations of whore.

She refused to undress. 'Smart bitch', one snarled, and they shoved her face down on the bonnet of the car and pulled her jeans and underclothes down, one holding her by the hair. What followed was obscene, violent and degrading.

She was numb with pain, fear – and concern for Angela, who was a virgin. And who, Donna thought guiltily, wouldn't be there except for her. She could hear her friend whimpering in the car. It rained again. She tried to block out what was happening by concentrating on the sky, the refinery tanks and the raindrops on the windscreen. Forever after, a wet windscreen has jolted her into remembering these unspeakable acts.

The rapists laughed and taunted Donna as they zipped up their flies. She dressed herself and got in the car with Angela, thinking it was over. It wasn't. The Torana went a few hundred metres and stopped. Waiting was another station wagon, a metallic, mocha-brown Ford with curtains in the back. There were two men in it – a tag team. The big guy dragged Angela out and ordered both girls into the Ford. He got in, too, as if he owned them. They drove off. Donna didn't see the Torana again, except in bad dreams.

She had no idea where they were until she saw a Footscray Institute of Technology sign as the car turned down a sloping entrance to parkland beside the river opposite Flemington racecourse, still crowded after the races. It was quiet on the Footscray bank, but a family was nearby trying to have a picnic, despite the weather. The girls were raped again. Donna could see the picnickers through the fogged-up windows. She willed them to realise what was happening and rescue them.

They drove off again. The gang leader put his arm around Angela in a grotesque parody of affection, as if she was his girlfriend. When the car stopped at traffic lights, he whispered in Donna's ear, 'I know you'd like to run'. They drove under a bluestone bridge where water was lying across the road, almost knee-deep. They turned into cobbled lanes among warehouses and factories, somewhere in North Melbourne or Kensington, went up a steep lane and stopped in a car park underneath a building. It was dark and deserted but suddenly the space was filled with the rumble of a V8 engine and male voices. More men.

Donna whispered to Angela to cling to the pack leader, 'Just stay with him – he won't let anyone else touch you.'

She was not sure this was true, or even if they would survive. She feared their ordeal was heading for some sinister climax: 'I was frightened we were going to be annihilated.' One by one, the newcomers raped Donna. Except the last one, the twelfth man to straddle her that day.

She saw his face. She thought one of the others called him 'Steve'. He was smaller and fairer than the rest and less sure of himself. She whispered to him, 'Help me get out of here.'

He quietly helped her get dressed, then called to the leader, 'Mate, it's getting late. Why don't we get rid of them?'

They drove. It was getting dark. Minutes later, the car pulled into a lane beside North Melbourne railway station. The girls were shoved out, like pieces of rubbish. They had avoided death but their life sentences were just beginning.

Donna's police statement trickled through the system and across the city from Nunawading to Footscray CIB, a crowded office with stained carpet and strained resources in one of the busiest police stations in Australia.

The file was handed to a detective who was transferred soon after, then to another, who was too busy on recent offences to waste time on something that happened so long ago. And so, in mid-1993, the file passed to Detective

Sergeant Richard Parsons, the constable at the 1976 Melbourne Cup.

Parsons had lived and worked in the western suburbs all his life and none knew 'the patch' better. He had seen a lot of bad endings but, unusual in his calling, that had not stopped him being calm and courteous. Only a fool would mistake this for weakness or lack of purpose. No policeman who has worked the Melbourne waterfront is a soft target – but it didn't stop him having a soft heart.

When Parsons read Donna's statement, it touched a nerve. He remembered gang rapes in the district in the 1970s and it bothered him that some went unsolved. Besides, he had a daughter of his own. And when he spoke to Donna, they struck a rapport.

Without new leads, there wasn't a lot Parsons could do, but he did what he could. The starting point was the man Donna knew as Wayne Thompson and his friend John. Although Wayne had lied that John was his brother, Donna knew his real surname. What she didn't know was that Wayne had also lied about his own surname: it wasn't Thompson.

The day after the rapes, Wayne had called her at home and told her his telephone had been disconnected and she would not be hearing from him. She had no idea where he worked, except that he was probably a labourer or apprentice tradesman. He had vanished.

Sergeant Parsons soon found John, who still lived locally. He had a string of convictions – assaults, thefts and drink driving – and had served time for armed robbery in the 1980s. The detective wasn't surprised when John denied having anything to do with Donna or the rapes.

On John's criminal record, Parsons noticed that one of his associates was called Wayne, though his surname was not Thompson. This Wayne (Wayne X) was the right age – 18 in 1976 – and had a record for assault, theft and burglary in the 1970s. He had served time in Turana youth training centre.

When Donna visited Melbourne in January, 1996, the detective showed her a series of mug shots of possible suspects, including a poor-quality photocopy of Wayne X. She paused over the picture and said the eyes reminded her of 'Wayne Thompson' but she wasn't sure.

Meanwhile, Parsons had traced Angela. Whereas Donna had left Melbourne soon after the rapes and had lived interstate ever since, Angela had stayed. They'd written to each other briefly but the friendship had petered out. They had little in common except their ordeal, which each had tried to bury in her own way.

Angela had married, had children and moved to an outer suburb. Parsons arranged to meet her discreetly. Angela confirmed Donna's statement but refused to be involved in any possible prosecution.

Her husband and children did not know about the rapes and she wanted it to stay that way.

It looked like a dead end.

In June 1996, Donna was going through things she had stuffed into a suitcase when leaving Melbourne 20 years before. She opened a satchel full of school English notes. As she put it down, something orange fell out.

It was a ticket to the 1976 Rocktober concert at Festival Hall. On the back was written 'Wayne' and a telephone number. She stared at it, then sat down and typed a fax to Parsons. 'You'll never guess what!' it began. 'I'm still shaking with excitement and amazement.' She was sure the old telephone number would lead to Wayne and unravel the rapists' identities. Eventually, it would, but for a long time the orange ticket was a red herring.

In the rush to computer databases in the 1980s and '90s, old telephone records and manual systems had not only been superseded, but destroyed. In 1976, a disconnected telephone number might have been used to trace someone who didn't want to be found. But in 1996, the same number seemed useless because it couldn't be crosschecked using modern data systems.

Months after finding the ticket, Donna saw an article

about old telephone directories for sale. It gave her an idea. She asked the State Library of Victoria to look up Wayne X's surname in the 1976 Melbourne directory to see if any subscriber of that name matched the number she had. None did.

Donna either had to give up or look for a needle in a haystack. She decided to look. In June, 1997, she asked Telstra to let her search an archival copy of the 1976 directory. She spent hours every week at her state's Telstra headquarters, poring over it. She took four months and 655,000 names to find the number.

Again, it seemed like a breakthrough.

The name listed for the number was T. Fennell, at 175 Millers Road, Altona. Perhaps Fennell was a friend or relative of Wayne's family? It had the allure of the unknown and it seemed to Donna and the detective that T. Fennell was the missing clue.

But when Sergeant Parsons went to 175 Millers Road, his heart sank. It was a block of flats that had been rented out to dozens of tenants over the years. No one knew of a T. Fennell. Parsons and Donna set up stories in local newspapers, appealing for help. None came.

The problem was that the 1976 telephone directory had been out-of-date. (In fact, respectable tenants called Tony and Doris Fennell had moved out of the Millers Road flat in December, 1974, but Fennell's name and outdated address and number had mistakenly stayed in the 1976 directory. Meanwhile, the number had been allocated to new subscribers: Wayne X's parents. There was no way of knowing this until the author finally traced Tony Fennell to a country district in eastern Victoria.)

For five years, however, it threw the investigation off course. Without Fennell, it seemed they couldn't prove a connection between the telephone number and Wayne X. As it turned out, when Fennell was found, he couldn't directly make that connection – but he provided valuable information by pointing out that Donna had searched the wrong telephone directory. There was still hope.

In 2003, on a rare visit to Melbourne, Donna went to see Richard Parsons. Once more they revisited the crime scenes, from Festival Hall to Altona to the Maribyrnong riverbank to North Melbourne. This time the detective had unearthed a good-quality photograph of Wayne X in the 1970s. Donna said it looked like the Wayne she had known – but she needed to be sure. Later, she went to the State Library and asked for the 1977 telephone directory. She eventually found the telephone number she had written on her concert ticket 26 years before.

Proof that 'Wayne Thompson' was really Wayne X.

Proof that the past can reach out.

The last chapter of Donna's story has not been written because it has not happened yet. The ending she hopes for is that the net will tighten around the men who planned and committed the pack rape of two terrified teenage girls all those years ago.

She knows they are out there. Time has disguises – thinning hair and thickening waists – but it cannot alter some things. If he's alive, the leader of the pack will still be tall and broad-shouldered and have a southern European accent and a domineering personality and that distinctive crease across the bridge of his nose. Time cannot alter the fact he used to go around with his mates in a spotless red two-door Torana and that he knew someone with a dark-brown Ford station wagon with vinyl bench seats and a column shift.

The Torana was the sort of car young men prized. Somewhere, photographs of it will be in an album. Somewhere, people will remember the car and who owned it in 1976. The rapists are not the only ones with secrets. Richard Parsons is sure Donna and Angela were not the only girls set up and raped who didn't go to the police because they felt compromised by the unspoken suggestion that they had somehow 'asked for it.'

Those frightened girls will be middle-aged women now. Old enough not to be scared anymore and to help each other fight back. Each will know something that counts. Some might even know who their attackers are or where they live.

Meanwhile, time is running out for the gang. The day will come when the patient Sergeant Parsons will knock on the door of a pale brick-veneer house in a suburb on Melbourne's western fringe. It's the house where Wayne X lives with a new woman.

The detective will pick his time – Wayne is a truck driver these days, and isn't always home.

What happens next is up to Wayne. He can help police. Or he can try to protect the members of the gang.

Wayne X knows what jail is like: he once did time for assault. He was young and reckless then. Now he has family reasons not to go back inside. Wayne's wife died recently and he has a young daughter to worry about. It won't be long before she's at high school and wanting to go out with boys.

Two women later came forward to tell police they were victims of the same gang. They identified several suspects as members of the gang, and police established that two of the wanted men had died. Victims' names have been changed.

CHAPTER 6
A SASHIMI DEAL

The language barrier blocked their attempts to explain they were not necessarily party to a conspiracy, but victims of one.

Most people in jail look as if they belong there. Chika Honda isn't one of them. A tiny, polite woman who was 36 when she arrived in Australia and 47 when she was finally released, she looked out of place behind bars not just because of her race – Japanese are almost unknown in Australian prisons – but in demeanour. She has none of the streetwise edge prisoners usually have. No scars, tattoos, or tattered ear lobes. And, bar the questionable charge on which she was convicted, no criminal history.

Which is one reason why, after serving 10 years of a 15-year sentence, Honda was finally paroled. At that time, she had nothing to gain by insisting that she is as innocent as she looks. But she did have something to lose. She was warned that attempting to publicise her case might jeopardise her release.

She sat in the contact visit room of the Dame Phyllis Frost Centre, a prison on Melbourne's western outskirts.

Her face lit up as she explained, in the broken English learned in jail, that she came to Australia to see kangaroos and koalas 10 years before, but had not seen any yet. She spoke of her conversion to Christianity and says her faith has sustained her through illness and despair that took her to the brink of suicide.

'I did not understand anything and it was like a dream,' she wrote in 1999, in a moving appeal translated by a supporter. 'I wanted to quickly wake up from the dream so many times that I tried to pinch my cheek and hit myself. But it was of no avail.

'It was not a dream... My heart has been hurt as if it has been stabbed with a knife.'

Her piece was headed *The Clear Voice of Miss Chika Honda*, which is presumably an attempt to label her honest and uncensored thoughts – but who could be sure? This ambiguity shows, even in a few words, how much is lost in translation from Japanese to English.

In a trial where millions of words are spoken, how many mistakes would be made?

Honda felt stronger than she had in the past. But she could not hide a sense of injustice. She believed that she and four Japanese travelling companions were victims of a miscarriage of justice – that they were wrongfully convicted of smuggling heroin in 1992.

Honda had no grievance against the Victorian prison system – only against the investigation and trial that put her inside it. And, of course, against the Malaysian crime syndicate she believes set up her and the others as expendable 'patsies'.

Long after there is any advantage in lying, and too late for the truth to mend her shattered life, she wanted their story told.

It starts in Japan in early 1992. Yoshio Katsuno, then 35, a former low-level member of the Japanese racketeer group the Yakuza, told friends and relatives he had been offered a cheap group holiday in Australia. A gesture, he said, from a Malaysian Chinese known as 'Charlie' who was embarrassed that Yoshio had been hurt in a car accident while visiting him on business. Yoshio bought seven discount return air tickets from Tokyo to Kuala Lumpur; Charlie paid for air tickets from Kuala Lumpur to Melbourne.

Why Charlie subsidised the group is unclear, but the fact he did so was not unusual. It is common in Asia for business associates to give and receive substantial gifts.

Yoshio invited, among others, his two older brothers, Mitsuo and Masaharu. They knew he had arranged a bargain holiday through business contacts and, because he had travelled before, he was willing to lead the group.

Travelling in groups with a leader is another common Japanese practice.

Mitsuo, then 36, had a thriving business clearing building sites. His brother Masaharu, then 42, was a retired police officer. Yoshio had once done prison time for street offences and possession of marijuana, which explained why the former policeman was estranged from him. Mitsuo, the middle brother, hoped the holiday would heal the rift.

Mitsuo invited his long-term girlfriend but when her work prevented her from going, he asked a mutual female friend, Chika Honda, to use the spare ticket.

Yoshio sold two of his tickets to a friend's firm that wanted to use the profits to save tax. The firm gave the tickets to an employee, Megumi Ishikubo; she invited a friend, Hiromi Kato. He also invited Kiichiro Asami, then 59, a former film stuntman.

None of the travellers knew everyone else in the group, but that wasn't unusual. Neither was their proposed five-day flying visit of Kuala Lumpur, Melbourne and Sydney.

The group's itinerary followed the usual tourist trail: bus tours to the penguins at Phillip Island, gold panning at Sovereign Hill and group visits to Captain Cook's Cottage, the Shrine of Remembrance and the MCG before going to Sydney for two days.

For all a prosecutor's later efforts to portray the visit as a sham, it was what bona fide Japanese tourists on a tight schedule usually do.

The group members met each other, most for the first time, just before they left Japan for Kuala Lumpur, where they were to have a one-night stopover and meet Yoshio's contact, Charlie, who was supposedly to go to Australia with them. Charlie met them at the airport in Kuala Lumpur with several other Malaysians, who ushered them to waiting cars – two sedans and a van.

Yoshio and the two women he knew, Kato and Ishikubo, had less luggage than the others and put it in the boot of one sedan. The other four – Honda, Asami, and the older Katsuno brothers – put their bags in the van.

Their story from this point was later ridiculed in court and depicted as a fabrication, but it has never wavered in any detail in a decade. They have always said they were driven to the Sakura Restaurant, where they ate dinner with Charlie. He had planned to fly to Melbourne with them, but said he had been delayed and would follow a day later. After dinner, they found the van had vanished from a nearby street, with the luggage in it. Charlie made a show of yelling at his men.

The luggage of three of them was in the boot of one of the sedans and was safe. But the other four, who had lost their luggage, were distraught. Because they couldn't speak Malay, they followed Charlie's instructions.

Charlie – oddly, in hindsight – told them he wouldn't call the police and that he would try to find the stolen luggage his own way. They all went to the Gentling Highlands resort apartments (already booked by Charlie) except Yoshio, who stayed to help search for the luggage.

Late that night, Charlie and Yoshio arrived at the resort to say they hadn't caught the thief, but they had found the luggage, which would be returned next day. But when the four came to fetch their gear next morning, instead of their own bags they found four large new suitcases.

Yoshio said their bags had been slashed open by the thief and were ruined, but that their clothes were unharmed and Charlie's men had repacked them in new suitcases.

Ten years later the other two women, Kato and Ishikubo, independently recalled Chika Honda's dismay in statements seen by the author. Honda was upset her bag had been slashed because it would have been so easy to open. And she complained that the new suitcase was too heavy.

Masaharu also disliked the suitcase because it was much harder to handle than the two soft bags he had lost. Significantly, he and Yoshio went shopping for replacement bags that day but he decided they were too expensive and he should look for a better buy in Melbourne.

In any case, Charlie's ever-obliging employees carried their luggage from the hotel to the cars and then to the airport check-in counter, so the weight of the suitcases didn't affect the four travellers too much.

Until they got to Melbourne, that is. Which they did at 6.35am on 17 June, 1992. If the Japanese tourists with four new suitcases knew what was hidden in them, they showed no sign of it, judging from the video recording their arrival and the initial search in the Customs hall.

All six look equally perplexed and annoyed at the delay – but not yet nervous, despite the fact that their tour leader, Yoshio, was obviously being questioned.

Even after X-rays revealed false panels in the four suitcases, and an electric drill revealed a narcotic powder, the Japanese seemed more confused than scared, reflecting a habitual trust in authority not yet shaken by events beyond their control.

There was much they didn't know then. About the extent to which the mysterious Charlie had orchestrated the trip, and why. And about his involvement with the Triad gangs, notorious heroin traffickers.

It was only later that the Japanese wondered why so many Federal Police had apparently been waiting when their flight landed before dawn. It transpired that Yoshio's visa had been cancelled while they were in transit, which led Customs and police to question him and then his travelling companions after he happily volunteered he was carrying their tickets and passports.

The fuss over Yoshio's visa seems, in hindsight, a routine way to mask a tip-off.

It wasn't as if sniffer dogs detected the suspect suitcases, or that Japanese were routinely targeted as likely heroin traffickers. So, if police were acting on information, as they almost invariably do, then who tipped them off, and why?

Was it set-up by Triad gangsters to harm a rival? Or was it an equally cold-blooded doublecross, a 'throw-off' to divert attention from a bigger drug importation on the same flight?

Either way, it relied on sacrificing the Japanese 'mules', regardless of whether all, any or none of them knew what was hidden in the substitute suitcases. Chika Honda, Asami and the Katsuno brothers would get years to brood about whether they were pawns in someone else's game. But on that June morning they were dazed and confused, trapped in every traveller's nightmare, though still confident their innocence would become obvious.

The evidence was damning but circumstantial. The language barrier compounded their plight, blocking the most rudimentary attempts to explain they were not necessarily party to a conspiracy, but victims of one.

Most damaging was the fact – soon leaked to a Melbourne newspaper – that their nominal tour leader had been linked to the Yakuza.

This prompted 'mafia' headlines, which confected great publicity for the Federal Police but jeopardised the chances of a fair jury trial for the rest of the group.

This concern was to be reinforced later, at the magistrates' court, when a small boy walked up to Masaharu and said: 'Japanese mafia'. The former policeman's heart sank because he knew then that a jury trial would be tainted by prejudice they didn't have the means to counter.

They could not speak enough English to communicate with their Legal Aid lawyers, let alone give proper evidence in their own defence. Worse, police had found it hard to find interpreters to conduct interviews and the result was a mess: meanings of questions and answers were so mangled in translation that, like a house built on quicksand, any trial relying on those interviews would be hopelessly compromised by its shaky foundations. No matter how conscientious the judge.

Before cases get to court, deals are done and compromises made for reasons that have little to do with truth or justice, more with winning and losing. The result can seem odd to outsiders. In this case, decades later, it still does.

One puzzle is why eight people were originally detained for conspiracy to smuggle heroin yet only six were charged, when the evidence seemed equally strong – or weak – in relation to all of them.

Initially detained were the seven Japanese and a Malaysian, Su Fonh Huat, who had been on the same flight, was booked into the same hotel, and who, it was alleged, was riding shotgun on the operation for Triads in Malaysia. Significantly, the airport 'pinch' on that Wednesday morning was kept secret until the following Sunday afternoon, when it was leaked in time to make headlines in Monday's newspapers.

There was a good reason for this delay: the police knew they didn't have the main player. In the missing four days, they had set up a 'controlled delivery' of the suitcases to a city hotel, hoping to trap whoever came to get the heroin. Teams of police were 'hidden' around the hotel, using the eight tourists as bait. Telephone lines were tapped and surveillance cameras set up.

The Japanese were so confident they were helping to catch the real culprits that Masaharu, using his own investigative experience, even suggested moving rooms to make surveillance easier – a suggestion the police adopted.

But Charlie did not land in Melbourne the day after the group, as he had promised. When no one else showed to collect the heroin, it was obvious the police operation was a flop. Someone must have warned Kuala Lumpur about the airport arrests.

This was a disappointment for the police. They had kilograms of heroin, but no charges laid. The irresistible suspicion is that, having failed to land the real trafficker, they made the best of a bad job by concentrating on the case against the Japanese 'mules', though not all of them.

Someone decided that the two women, Kato and Ishikubo, should return to Japan without being charged – presumably because they were lucky enough not to have been actually carrying the 'loaded' suitcases. While the other six were effectively under house arrest at the hotel, two policemen found time to take Kato and Ishikubo sightseeing to the zoo and the beach, in between long interrogations. Then they were sent home.

Interestingly, the two women later never wavered in backing the innocence of the other Japanese, but they were warned off returning to Australia to give evidence for the defence because (they both stated later) an Australian 'attorney' threatened they could also be charged if they did. Someone thought they might jeopardise a rickety prosecution. Which, of course, underlined the weak case against those unlucky enough to have received the suitcases. If Kato and Ishikubo could be arbitrarily judged not to be part of a conspiracy, then the same could be argued for Chika Honda and, by extension, all the Japanese. If any two could be cleared of knowing there was heroin in the cases, it follows that any – or all – could be similarly ignorant.

The decision to release the other two women was especially cruel for Honda. She had been a late inclusion to the tour and she didn't know Yoshio – who had an image problem: with his colourful body tattoos and chequered past, he was a star candidate for the lead role in the absence of the missing Triad mastermind.

If, after two years, several million words and almost as many dollars, the case against the Japanese tourists rested on one thing, it was this: a jury had to believe they were lying about their luggage being stolen.

Had the Japanese been able to support their story in any way, they stood to get the benefit of the doubt. It would be reasonable to believe they would accept new suitcases to replace stolen ones.

But the Japanese were defended by Legal Aid lawyers, who couldn't communicate with them easily, let alone afford any independent investigation in Malaysia to substantiate their story.

The prosecution, however, had no such problems. It arranged for a Malaysian policeman to interview staff at the restaurant. The policeman produced statements from a waiter and a car park attendant which, taken at face value, indicated the Japanese had not been there on the evening of 15 June, 1992, and that no vehicle had been stolen from the restaurant car park.

Those flimsy statements were enough, in the hands of a skilful prosecutor, to help persuade the jury to reject the Japanese's version of events and find them (and Su) guilty. Su and Yoshio were sentenced to 25 years' prison, later reduced on appeal to 20 years. Chika Honda and the other three men were sentenced to 15 years.

The waiter's statement, taken two months after the Melbourne arrests, does not refer to any table booking records – only to bills. The waiter states 'none of the bills indicate that a group of Japanese dined at the restaurant on that night'.

On what basis he makes this assertion is unclear: could he really recall the ethnicity of customers by the food they ordered? And even if there was a formal booking system – which there wasn't – it would be bizarre to note the race of customers, rather than the number of chairs needed. The suspicion is that the staff gave the answers the policeman wanted to hear.

Why? The answer, says an Australian lawyer who went to Malaysia last year to investigate, is that the restaurant is controlled by the Triad group that set up the heroin scam, and that the gang has influence in the Malaysian police force.

These are serious claims. The man who makes them was a serious man, an unlikely saviour for a group of Asians accused of heroin trafficking. At the time, Brian Erwin was a humble 63-year-old suburban lawyer in Sydney, semi-retired because of poor health.

He heard about Honda, Asami and the Katsuno brothers by chance from a Japanese-born lawyer as they waited together outside court. The lawyer had read about the case in a Japanese magazine her father had sent her.

Erwin was intrigued to find he and most Australians had never heard of a case regarded as a scandalous injustice in Japan, where 'the Melbourne incident' receives wide coverage. He decided to help.

Through Melbourne's small Japanese community, he found a group of supporters who visited the prisoners and made representations on their behalf to both Australian and Japanese authorities. Some of the supporters were Japanese who attend the Canterbury Presbyterian church.

They and others have devoted themselves to the case for years, raising money with bazaars and cake stalls.

The minister then at the church, Stephen Young, was an American citizen born in Japan and speaks Japanese fluently. Young, who later moved to Perth, pushed the prisoners' cause for ten years, convinced they were all innocent. He had contacts in Malaysia and, when Erwin offered to go there, gave him some leads.

Erwin spoke to a reformed Triad member willing to share his inside knowledge. He told Erwin that Charlie had Triad connections, and that the Sakura Restaurant was controlled by a Triad group.

He also introduced Erwin to a person whose identity cannot be published for fear of reprisals, who worked next to the restaurant and who recalled a loud (staged) disagreement between Charlie and his men in the street over the van being supposedly stolen.

Erwin ate at the restaurant and found it did not record bookings in any systematic way. He established that the van had been taken from a nearby lane, not from the car park.

But the most vital evidence he found was that the police officer who had taken the statements had been exiled to a one-man police station in the provinces after being accused of corruption.

Back in Australia, Erwin combed through the trial transcripts and witness statements, using his legal knowledge to look for inconsistencies. He found plenty, as did two private investigators paid to work on the case by the supporter group.

The police had little to link Yoshio and his unsuspecting Japanese group with the supposed Triad 'minder' Su. Key evidence was given at the trial by a telephonist from the Swanston Hotel that the same Asian male voice had, on separate calls, asked for both Su and Yoshio.

Erwin and Stephen Young believe the 'voice' was in fact two voices – one calling Su from Malaysia, the other being the Japanese consul in Melbourne, asking for Yoshio.

It's odd, noted Erwin drily, that the telephonist heard background noise on one call, which she recognised as trams rattling past. There are no trams in Kuala Lumpur but there were in St Kilda Road, outside the Japanese Consulate.

Everybody claims innocence when they first get to jail, prison wisdom goes, but only the truly innocent or the mentally deluded still claim it at the end of their sentences.

Even then, few are believed. Which makes the following anecdote all the more surprising.

When Brian Erwin first visited the male Japanese prisoners at Fulham, near Sale, he was surprised how friendly the prison officer escorting him was when Erwin said he was visiting the Japanese. The officer turned to him and said: 'They didn't do it, you know.'

The jail grapevine works fast. A minute later on, a tough prisoner covered in tattoos saw Erwin walk past and called out: 'They're not guilty.'

The line between guilty drug trafficker and innocent dupe is dangerously fine. That was highlighted in the case in which the then high-profile criminal lawyer Andrew Fraser and two co-conspirators were sentenced to long jail terms for smuggling cocaine into Australia.

The disgraced solicitor and Werner Roberts and Carl Heinze Urbanec were imprisoned after a trial in which the court accepted that Roberts had cynically set up his former girlfriend, Carol Brand, to carry cocaine into Australia without her knowledge.

But had it not been for police listening devices that recorded conversations between Roberts and Brand after they arrived in Sydney in late 1999, she would almost certainly have also been convicted and jailed as a conspirator. She had carried African wall plaques through Customs which, unknown to her, were filled with cocaine.

Police charged Brand, but her defence counsel, Paul Galbally, used transcripts of conversations recorded from listening devices to show she was an innocent dupe — that Roberts had lured her overseas by pretending he wanted to resume their previous relationship.

'Her story is quite chilling,' Galbally says. 'What happened to her is traumatic and Kafkaesque. Had there not been listening devices, it's unlikely anyone would have believed her. She was used in such a manipulative fashion that even at the point of arrest she didn't realise what had happened.

'Juries are cynical and conservative. The accused are stigmatised by the charge and have to prove they don't know about the drugs. Here was a woman with a good job whose only mistake was to go overseas with a married man, yet she could have ended up sentenced to 15 years' jail.'

That case has particular relevance to the plight of the Japanese convicted of heroin trafficking because it shows that people can be charged even when police have evidence that could clear them.

'Some of the investigators in this case must have known there was a very big question mark over Carol Brand's involvement,' Galbally says. But she and her lawyer and the judge all spoke the same language and so the truth came out. Chika Honda and her friends were not so lucky.

Chika Honda returned to Japan in 2002. In 2005 she was refused a visa to return to Australia see a stage show inspired by her ordeal: 'Chika, a documentary performance'. In Japanese legal and media circles the 'Melbourne case' has long been regarded as a scandalous injustice that reflects badly on the Australian legal system and Federal Police.

CHAPTER 7
THE ONE THAT GOT AWAY

'The cleverest crim I've ever met.'

David McMillan checked out of the 'Bangkok Hilton' late on a hot August night in 1996. As jailbreaks go, it was pure Hollywood.

No one had successfully broken out of Klong Prem prison in living memory. The most recent attempt had been 12 years before, when a Thai prisoner almost died trying.

The story goes like this: McMillan, 40, is sharing a cell with four Thai prisoners on the first floor of a two-storey block. He weakens the window bars with acid, breaks them, squeezes his lean frame through the tiny gap and lowers himself five metres to the ground, using electrical flex.

He slips past the prison dining hall and, conveniently, a sleeping guard. He retrieves a hidden bamboo ladder and scales the inner five metre wall, cuts barbed wire with wire cutters, crawls under coiled razor wire, drops to the other side.

Bolder now, he runs across the prison hospital grounds and scales an outer wall topped with electrified cables, unharmed. Oddly, no one in the watchtowers sees him jump down, then swim across a stinking canal that forms a moat around the notorious jail. He reaches the other side and a waiting accomplice.

Next day, as headlines about the audacious escape roll off the presses back in Australia, heads roll in the prison. McMillan's cellmates are beaten for colluding with him; prison officers face disciplinary action for 'carelessness'.

Eight remaining Australian prisoners get leg chains and lose privileges.

Meanwhile, in hiding, the only Westerner ever to escape from Klong Prem plans his next move.

Fade to black…

Caulfield Grammar has produced its share of the worthy and the notable – lord mayors, captains of industry, leaders in business and bureaucracy, politics and the professions, respected members of rowing clubs, racing clubs and Rotary clubs. But even the best schools have their wayward sons.

In Caulfield's case, there is the late Christopher Skase, who flew high, dreamed of being a film mogul, then fell to Earth – exposed as a flim-flam man, disgraced and died in exile. And there is Nick Cave, the Lou Reed of Wangaratta, whose musical and lyrical brilliance survived the dark influence of drugs to make his mark in the wider world.

Then there is David Peter McMillan. AKA Westlake, Dearing, Poulter, Magilton, Rayner, Elton, Knox, Hunter and many more aliases.

McMillan, like his two more famous schoolmates, is a long way from home these days.

That is, as far as anyone knows. At the time of writing, few know where he is, and those who might know become suddenly vague when the subject is raised. Which is not surprising, given that he's a wanted man who, technically, faces a death sentence in Thailand and years of jail time in Australia if he's caught.

Like the young Skase, McMillan was a dreamer and a schemer with an eye for the main chance, an ear for information and a head for figures. Like Cave, he was a restless, creative spirit drawn to the dark side. His undoing was that he succumbed to the worst of both impulses – the desire for fast money and the weakness for drugs.

McMillan – bright, ambitious and a heroin user – was in his early twenties when he decided to get in on the ground floor of a growth industry. Instead of getting into computers or honing his natural talents as a photographer, cameraman and writer, he became a drug trafficker. At least, that's the prosecution case against him; McMillan, always a good talker, swore he was a harmless addict who subsidised his habit with a little gold and gemstone smuggling.

A jury almost believed him – acquitting him of all but one charge of conspiracy to import heroin – but the judge was not so sympathetic, sentencing him and two accomplices to 17 years in prison, to the delight of the police taskforce that had matched wits with the McMillan crew for months. A disgruntled defence lawyer said later that the sentence was as severe as if they had been convicted of all 12 charges, not one.

The year was 1983. The trial of McMillan and his associates – a former Olympic standard athlete, Michael Sullivan, and a Thai national called Supahaus Chowdury – ran for almost six months, and it took the jury a record eight days to reach its 'little bit guilty' verdict.

It was, then, the longest and most expensive criminal trial in Victorian legal history – and, while the result must have disappointed McMillan, it clearly didn't surprise him. Before the trial had even begun, he had orchestrated an audacious plan from his cell, to escape from Pentridge Prison in a hijacked helicopter, the first leg of a plan involving heavy disguises, an interstate truck ride hidden in cargo, a sea-going boat and a light plane. The police were tipped off and foiled what would have been another surreal episode in the existence of a man who lived his life as if it were a screenplay, with himself playing an anti-hero... the sort of lovable rogue who's supposed to get the girl, the money and the last laugh over bumbling authority. The real story is a little bleaker.

Films always fascinated David McMillan. As a boy, he earned schoolyard fame presenting the 'Peters Junior News' on television. After switching from Prahran High to Caulfield Grammar mid-way through secondary school, he directed and starred in an action movie spoof his classmates still smile about, decades later. It's as if, says a lawyer who once represented him and became his friend, he is unable to separate real life from the reel unspooling in his mind.

For someone who impressed most people he met as charming, clever and generous, the young McMillan developed – or affected – some bad habits early in life.

When he arrived at Caulfield Grammar in fourth form in 1971 – the form above Nick Cave – he seemed, one former classmate recalls, 'from another world'.

The teenage McMillan didn't blend in. Or he didn't want to. By an accident of birth – he was born overseas and his parents were divorced – he was different in ways he didn't try to hide, from his smart accent to his subversive attitude. It struck some of his classmates later that his cultivation of differences between himself and the herd was an affectation that came to define his character and behaviour. Others might work hard and obey the rules, but he was too cool for such bourgeois stuff.

Born to an Australian expatriate couple who worked in British radio and television before separating, he had arrived in Australia as a child with his mother (and her new husband), his sister and younger half-brother.

Where others, given the same start, might have soon blended with the majority, McMillan didn't just guard his outsider status, but promoted it. He impressed some people more than he did others, but they all agreed on one thing: he loved beating the system.

He inherited charm, talent and looks from his mother, a stylish, attractive and worldly woman regarded with some awe by his classmates, who thought her (as one put it later) 'a bit more glamorous than our mothers, with a cheeky sense of humour'.

While most families lived conventional nine-to-five lives in conventional suburban homes, McMillan lived in an apartment in Alma Road, St Kilda. There was a whiff of bohemia about his home life that fascinated his schoolmates, whose horizons, then, didn't extend far beyond the Yarra. A few of them visited the flat at lunchtimes or after school, and glimpsed insights into a teenager who fancied notoriety and the best things money could buy.

One contemporary recalls McMillan boasting that his mother was close to the then controversial abortionist, Dr J.G.A. Troup, 'which was quite out of our league'. Another remembers his enviable record collection – every disc a coveted 'import'.

He was a 'big noter' with champagne tastes, and he cut corners to get what he wanted. A couple of examples have stuck in memories for almost three decades.

'He was a dodgy bugger,' recalls a bemused Paul Tankard of his one-time classmate. 'He gave the impression of living life on the edge. He made a practice of going into the school canteen by the side door, and saying he was there to get lunch for a teacher – a "Mr Wilson" – so that he would not only bypass the queue but get a free lunch.' Tankard and another classmate, Pater Cole, scripted the short film McMillan was to direct, shoot and act in. Tankard recalls McMillan boasting he had obtained the film stock by using a credit card he had 'found'. The question is: did he commit this small fraud – or just convince his friends that he had? A lie, either way.

'You knew you couldn't rely on him and that he wasn't a good influence,' Tankard concludes tolerantly. 'But he was ever interesting.'

McMillan was one of a small group that put together the school's student newspaper, a rather more raffish publication than the official school publication, *The Grammarian*. That an artistic classmate, Peter Grant, drew a caricature of him for the newspaper, emphasised his maverick image. He didn't bother with the usual sporting and academic endeavours and so there is only one photograph of him in the magazine. In it, he sits at the centre of a group, a cloud of dark curls around his lean face – holding a copy of *MAD* magazine in front of him, as he looks coolly at the camera.

Not everyone fell for McMillan's winning ways. A veteran housemaster, 'Kanga' Corden, took Paul Tankard aside one day and warned 'that I wasn't doing myself any favours hanging around with the likes of McMillan. Kanga had McMillan's number, all right.'

Word must have spread in the staff room because, at the end of fifth form, McMillan vanished. His mates returned to Caulfield for their final year, but someone had quietly told him not to. Reasons for this were never made public.

But, in the new year of 1973, the consensus was that it was something to do with drugs. In light of later developments, that seems likely.

Taylor's College was, and is, a Melbourne institution in both senses of the word. For years, it has offered an alternative route to tertiary education for those prepared to pay – and who, for various reasons, do not study elsewhere.

Among Taylor's annual intakes of hardworking students was a sprinkling of more colourful characters who have rebelled against mainstream education. Some of these were failures having another try; others had been expelled or had left elsewhere under a cloud. In the class of 1973, David McMillan fell into this category. The following year it was a tough kid from Marcellin College called Alphonse Gangitano, later to become a notorious gangster and, later still, a dead one, shot by an underworld associate.

McMillan was never going to be a gunman. It wasn't his style. But, for all his intelligence, he wasn't destined for an academic career either. He skipped classes, forged passes, and that was the end of his formal education. At 17, he was picked up for passing dud cheques and was already on a road leading to what a lawyer friend later wryly described as 'his *Midnight Express* life'.

An eclectic and voracious reader, McMillan devoured information he thought he could use. The boy who'd duped the school tuckshop was graduating to the big time, still by trying to beat the system.

He was later to try the more cerebral criminal arts – forgery, disguise, fraud and smuggling – but, at bottom, he was a confidence man. Everything else he did was based on his ability to befriend and to deceive. But, like all con artists, he had to convince himself before he could convince others. If he imagined himself as a character from *Day of The Jackal*, there was also some Walter Mitty in his readiness to lace reality with fantasy. It's hard to know where one starts and the other ends.

There are people in Melbourne – sensible people at the top of their professions – who firmly believe that McMillan was a misguided genius, who was, however briefly, a whiz kid in the advertising industry in his early twenties. Proof of this, they claim, is that he was the creative force behind several well-known television advertisements in the mid-to-late 1970s.

Whether McMillan even worked in advertising at all is a moot point – and, if he did, he was never prominent. People in the industry don't remember him, and yet he told friends he'd been responsible for successful Mars Bar and RC Cola commercials, among others. A close relative also remembers things differently, saying he had never held down a job for long, even if his knowledge of photography and film might have won him enough work on the fringes of advertising to weave a believable tale from a thread of truth. The truth, says the relative grimly, is that his greatest talent was using deception to avoid work.

'He was very kind in some ways, but cruel in others –

and always a shocking liar. He was always trying to con other people and was very lazy.' An example: as a primary school student he was offered pocket money to weed the garden, but he immediately tried to persuade a neighbour's child to do the chore for him – at a reduced rate. He didn't want the work, only the profit. 'And he got caught doing it,' says the relative. 'That sums him up.'

Long after the wily old policeman had retired from 'The Job' and taken up bowls, they still used him as an example to recruits of how curiosity and alertness can crack a case wide open.

The lesson went like so. Back in 1980, like neighbours everywhere, the policeman was curious about the new people in the house next-door. They were young, good looking, smart – and conspicuous spenders. The woman drove a Porsche and her boyfriend a Fiat. They had friends with a late-model Rover, an Alfa Romeo and a big American car, and they came and went at all times of the day and night. Glance through a window and you'd glimpse the latest in electrical gear and cameras.

Then there was the landscaping and the renovations – even in an affluent Melbourne bayside suburb like this, it seemed like over-capitalising. A sign, perhaps, like the 'grass castles' in the vineyards of Mildura and Griffith, of black money with nowhere else to go.

But the really suspicious thing about the people next door, it seemed to the old cop, was that they didn't seem to work. They would disappear for days or weeks at a time, but when they returned, they lived the indolent lives of spoiled teenagers with bottomless allowances. Late to bed, late to rise, eating out most nights. Their main past time was to amuse themselves, it seemed to him.

The policeman started jotting down car registration numbers, and running the usual checks on the names that came up. He passed his suspicions on, up the chain of command.

First came the surveillance and the intelligence gathering. The policeman's nomadic neighbours were near enough to 'cleanskins', but if they lacked criminal records, they were on the way to getting them. For a start, they were using heroin – and dealing in it to support not only their habits, but their affluence. It was soon clear they had more than cars and cameras – they had properties everywhere.

Heroin brought them into contact with people for whom treachery was a way to survive. It was only a matter of time before a word was dropped discreetly, in an interview room, in return for bail or a blind eye. And the word was that the private school crew with the European cars did more than use the stuff and sell it to others. They were importing it.

In 1979, Australia's drug scene was tiny compared with

what it would be two decades later. Heroin was scarce, prices high and 'street' purity low. The potential for profit was huge. For anyone with the nerve – and no conscience – it was tempting.

David McMillan had never been one to resist temptation. Even his fondest admirers would admit that. Few outside family and close friends knew it, but when he had visited Britain soon after leaving school, he served several months in Reading Jail. His tools were forgery, false identities and fraud. His aim was smuggling – although, whereas he would later insist he was smuggling gold and gems to feed his growing drug habit, the evidence would indicate a far more valuable contraband.

McMillan's girlfriend was Clelia Vigano, daughter of the well-known hotelier and restaurateur Ferdie Vigano. Clelia's grandfather, Mario Vigano, had married a European countess, was the proprietor of the original Mario's restaurant in Exhibition Street, and had prospered so that the family became a Melbourne institution. But Clelia, beautiful but doomed, fell into – or was attracted by – bad company. She and McMillan shared an addiction to heroin and high living, that was to cost him years in prison – and Clelia her life.

That was later. In 1979 McMillan, then 24, was bursting with confidence. He had teamed up with Michael Sullivan, who was several years older but, like McMillan, a middle-class heroin addict with few of the obvious markers of criminal behaviour, but all of the instincts.

Sullivan had been a champion schoolboy pole vaulter whose veteran coach, Wal Chisholm, considered the best athlete he'd trained in 40 years. Sullivan beat the Commonwealth medal winner when still a teenager, was the first Australian to clear 16 feet and qualified for the Mexico Olympics in 1968, but missed selection in favour of older competitors.

'If he'd got to Mexico he would have won a medal at Munich (in 1972). He was such a tremendous competitor,' muses the old coach, who still sticks up for his one-time teenage prodigy, although he admits the young Sullivan was as happy to go surfing as train. Then came an ankle injury that ended his career and started a depression that only heroin seemed to help. By the time he met McMillan, he was an addict who dreamed of easy money.

Tim Egan, a detective who was to match wits with the pair for months, says: 'These were conmen-cum-commodity dealers who realised that a kilo of gold might be worth $29,000 but a kilo of heroin was worth $290,000. Their key personal characteristic was arrogance. They worked on the principle that their phones were tapped – but they kept going anyway.'

McMillan perfected a way to beat the passport and airline ticketing system, which, before computers were used, still relied on manual filing. He haunted the newspaper archives at the State Library, where he scoured 1950s death notices for the names of infants whose age would roughly correspond with himself or his friends. Then – either personally or by sending someone else – he applied for copies of birth certificates in the dead children's names. Because there was no cross-referencing of births with deaths, these could be used to apply for passports once he had established other fake, proof of identification material – student ID cards, credit cards and the like.

McMillan had what some considered a freakish ability to absorb information. He all but memorised a book of international flight schedules obtained from a travel agent, allowing him to devise complicated routes to exploit busy periods and cut the risk of Customs searches.

He befriended a city travel agent, and bought multiple sets of tickets in different names so he and his couriers could switch identities halfway through a trip.

With multiple passports and double sets of tickets, McMillan would land in Bangkok for a few days, buy cheap high-grade heroin, seal it in a specially made stereo tuner and hand it to his courier. Then, using fresh passports and tickets, the pair would fly on separately to a European destination – often London – not regarded as a likely source of illicit narcotics, before returning to Australia using the original tickets and passports.

The aim of this elaborate ruse was to present at Australian Customs – always at a busy time, usually in Sydney – using passports with no sign of an Asian stopover of the sort that attracted attention.

It worked well for a while. Between March 1980 and April 1981, McMillan orchestrated seven courier runs through Bangkok to Europe and back. Then he found that drug smuggling and drug using don't mix.

McMillan's 'mule' on that trip was a drug addict called Mark Anthony Jordan. The police reconstruction of what happened is that, in Bangkok, McMillan handed Jordan a stereo tuner with 1.692 kilograms of heroin packed into its casing. Jordan was high on heroin, but, instead of aborting the European leg of the journey, they went ahead.

Jordan was obviously drug affected and, at the airport, he was detained and searched. McMillan, using the name William Knox, flew on. He was apprehended by the Belgian police in Brussels, and held for 24 hours, but was released and went to London, where he met another courier, a Melbourne gardener called Peter. Days later, using another alias, McMillan flew via Amsterdam to New Zealand – then back to Australia, via Brisbane.

Jordan was rotting in a Thai jail (where he would eventually die) and McMillan had avoided the same fate by a whisker. If he'd retired then, he might have got away with it forever. He knew he was a marked man, but he didn't turn over a new leaf – just a new angle.

Enter Supahaus Chowdury, Thai drug supplier. Days after getting home McMillan, Sullivan, Clelia Vigano and Sullivan's de facto wife, a Colombian called Mary Escolar Castilo, were introduced to Chowdury by a Melbourne drug dealer.

In the following months, McMillan had a special antenna installed at Sullivan's house in Brighton, like those at his own houses in Brighton and Beaumaris. This let them use powerful radios and scanners to communicate secretly – and monitor police messages.

The police were also preparing. The Chief Commissioner, Mick Miller, called in the head of the drug squad, Geoff Baker, and another senior policeman, and proposed a joint taskforce with the Federal Police and Customs. The taskforce, codenamed Operation Aries, had more than 20 investigators and a secret inner-suburban headquarters. It was the first time Victorian police had finally worked with 'The Feds' and Customs.

Warrants were drawn, telephone taps and 'bugs' installed, and surveillance teams set loose. McMillan and

Sullivan must have suspected they were being watched; it didn't stop them. Detectives recall how McMillan, so careful in other ways, would brazenly double-park his car in the city and wander around the streets, carrying a plastic bag full of cash, buying whatever took his fancy.

In November, Chowdury called to say he was coming from Bangkok. Sullivan warned him to land with a tour group at a busy time.

He did – on 4 December, 1981. But investigators were watching him. In Melbourne, Customs x-rayed two ornate cutlery boxes he was carrying in a carpet bag, but found no abnormality. He went to the Southern Cross Hotel; the police were in the next room with a listening device. After midnight, he took a taxi to meet McMillan and Sullivan in Brighton. The police sneaked into his room, drilled a hole in one of the cutlery boxes, and found heroin.

McMillan and Sullivan knew they were being watched, but played on. 'It was a game to McMillan,' recalls Geoff Baker, now long-retired from the drug squad. 'He was an egotist. You could read his mind: "I'll take them on".'

Next day, Chowdury went to Mercy Maternity Hospital, carrying the cutlery boxes in a bag, and met McMillan in the foyer – sitting next to an undercover policeman. It was a cunning move, because police would be reluctant to open fire there.

Suddenly, Sullivan drove into a lane near the foyer, McMillan and Chowdury ran to meet him, and McMillan tossed the bag through the open car window. Sullivan reversed, almost running over hospital visitors, and sped off. Chowdury and McMillan walked to McMillan's Fiat as police chased the Rover. Both vehicles, and an Alfa Romeo driven by Mary Escolar Castilo, were lost.

All the police had was a drill with some heroin powder on it. But it would be enough.

On Christmas Day, three weeks later, Chowdury landed in Perth, flew to Sydney, stayed in King's Cross, flew to Canberra and caught a bus to Melbourne. Police followed him all the way. They arrested him at 2.37am on 27 December. He said little and wouldn't sign a record of interview. Ironically, he was there to get his money, not to smuggle more drugs.

Meanwhile, Thai police were searching Chowdury's houses in Thailand. They found bags of heroin, raw opium, partly constructed cutlery boxes and a press for compressing drugs.

Detectives raided McMillan's Beaumaris house at dawn on 5 January, 1982. They found him and Vigano in bed, a packet of heroin, $8000 cash, scales, a grinder and other drug gear. McMillan denied knowing Chowdury and said 'no comment' when asked about the maternity hospital episode.

In Brighton, Sullivan and Castilo were also in bed. Police found photographs of Chowdury and Sullivan together. Sullivan claimed Chowdury had given him 'presents' at the hospital four weeks before.

Next day, police took McMillan to a house he owned in Carlton and found a plastic bag with $69,930 sitting on a wardrobe – as much, then, as the house was worth. It helped explain why McMillan had such good information – he could buy it.

For, besides drugs and money, the detectives had found something else a list in McMillan's neat handwriting, naming every taskforce member.

While they had been watching him, he'd been watching them.

A month later, Clelia Vigano and Mary Escolar Castilo were dead – killed in a fire that Vigano and another prisoner, Danielle Wright, apparently lit at Fairlea Women's Prison.

It seemed a sinister coincidence that two women who could have given damning evidence against McMillan and Sullivan were dead. But a coroner found later that Vigano and Wright's 'gross recklessness' had killed Castilo. There was nothing to support the Vigano family's suspicions that it was pre meditated murder.

Ten months after the Fairlea fire, police heard a whisper

about a plot to spring McMillan and Sullivan' from Pentridge by helicopter. A transport operator told a policeman he'd been offered a huge amount to move escapees hidden on the back of a truck. Detectives traced a former British soldier, Percival Hole, who had come from the Philippines after being approached by Sullivan's sister, Norma.

Police monitored Hole's hotel room, and heard him boasting of a plan to land a helicopter on the prison tennis court, drop the escapees in a park, take them to a flat where waiting make-up artists would disguise them, then hide them in crates that would be trucked to Queensland. This would be followed by another truck carrying an ocean-going boat, in case of emergencies, and would meet a light plane that would fly them to the Philippines, where Sullivan's sister had connections with the Marcos regime.

The plan was smashed. Hole and McMillan's go-between, his accountant Max McCready, were arrested and jailed. Police who re-enacted the scheme insisted it would have worked, had Hole kept quiet and found a helicopter. And if it all sounded like something out of a film, it was a Charles Bronson thriller called *Break Out*.

McMillan did his time easily; Sullivan didn't. Chowdury worked in the Pentridge kitchens and reportedly donated $18,000 of equipment to the jail when he won early release after ten years.

McMillan and Sullivan were also generous benefactors to the prison system, according to jail gossip. Rumour has it that a swimming pool built by Builders Laborers Federation members (after union boss Norm Gallagher served time) used $30,000 of materials paid for by anonymous benefactors connected with the pair.

Although popular with police and prison officers, McMillan was not as well-liked by fellow prisoners. He and Sullivan were regarded as 'yuppie crims' who got favourable treatment.

Although sentenced to 17 years in August 1983, McMillan was given day-leave from jail by 1991. His charisma – and network of contacts – was such that *The Financial Review* published a flowery piece he wrote about his first day on leave from prison.

He dined out with his family and, on another leave pass, with his former defence lawyer, who now considered him a friend. And he was making plans for a fresh start. He impressed one of Melbourne's better-known actors that he had a story to tell.

Later, when he was released on licence, McMillan visited the actor at his beach house. 'When he came to see me, supposedly to discuss writing a book,' the actor mused later, 'he already had a new car and a mobile phone. I should have realised that writing would be too boring for him.'

Police, however, weren't as trusting as family and friends. A Romanian who'd known McMillan in prison told an undercover policeman he was 'the cleverest crim I've ever met' and hinted that his plans didn't include writing for a living.

While maintaining an innocent facade, McMillan was busy. Police later heard he was buying rock heroin from other traffickers, crushing it and moulding it into uniform 'discs', complete with a brand stamped on it. He then spread the fiction that it was the latest and purest heroin on the market. Buyers swamped him.

'It was just a brilliant marketing trick,' says the undercover policeman, who had seen gangsters at work for years. Just before Christmas 1993, McMillan was arrested in Bangkok after running from an airline clerk who questioned his passport. The passport was false, and half-a-kilogram of heroin was hidden in his luggage. Procedures had changed since the 1980s, and McMillan hadn't caught up. '

Three years later, he had made enough friends inside and outside prison to go out the window and over two walls. And since?

Word filtered to Melbourne a few months later that he had been arrested on the Afghanistan-Pakistan border. But, somehow, he'd persuaded – or bribed – the authorities to let him go, then vanished.

He'd be delighted to know – if he doesn't already – that there is little to stop him slipping back to Victoria. Not only is there no warrant for his arrest known to state police but the force doesn't even have a photograph of him on file. Obviously just another lucky break, like the night he skipped Klong Prem prison. Or is it?

McMillan, 60, was released from a British prison in early 2017, vowing never to return. He said he was relieved that Thailand had finally formally dropped its claim to extradite him back to the country where he faced the death sentence.

CHAPTER 8
THE SUICIDE THAT WASN'T

Blood's thicker than water. That's one reason it's so hard to wash away.

For anyone callous enough to pull the trigger, shooting Jennifer Tanner wasn't the problem. Making it look like suicide was, and that's where her killer got it wrong. Faking suicide meant using the only firearm available to the victim: her husband's bolt-action .22 rifle. When the first shot didn't kill the terrified woman instantly, the self-appointed executioner had to fire another shot into her forehead as her body twitched and thrashed.

In fact, the killer almost certainly fired even more shots on that Wednesday night in November, 1984. If he did, they missed. At least, they missed her head. When Laurie Tanner came home and found his wife's body he didn't notice the bullet holes through both hands, but they were there: the sort experts call 'classic defence wounds'.

All of which, you'd think, would make it likely that someone might consider foul play…

Even if the pair of country policemen first called to the Tanners' house at Bonnie Doon were fooled by the fact

Jennifer's body was slumped on a couch with the rifle between her knees, the muzzle pointing towards her still-bleeding head.

Even if a local doctor dragged from a dinner party agreed it looked like suicide, pronounced life extinct and left, pointing out later it was his job to verify death, not to investigate its causes.

And even if the detective sergeant on call that night ignored alarm signals when the uneasy constables telephoned him again after finding a second bullet shell near the body. Detective Sergeant Ian Welch, known locally as 'Columbo', stuck to his original decision not to make the long drive to attend, nor to bother with fingerprinting or forensic tests.

Even photographs were ruled out, which was lucky for the accredited police photographer on duty that night, a Sergeant Neil Phipps. Despite being rostered on, Phipps had left Mansfield police station to attend to private affairs.

And so the die was cast. The word 'suicide' – repeated to each new person introduced to the case – settled over the tragedy, shrouding the truth. Bill Kerr, older of the two uniformed policemen at the scene, knew more about traffic fines than shootings. But some things niggled him. Such as the half-drunk cup of coffee and plate of biscuits near Jennifer Tanner's body. And the fact she had asked her husband to bring home a local paper, milk, bread and a 'surprise' – a chocolate bar. It hardly seemed the behaviour of a suicidal woman.

There was, too, the fact her 21-month-old son was alone in the house. What mother, if not actually deranged, would suicide without making sure her baby was taken care of first? There was no evidence Jenny was deranged. And she hadn't left a suicide note. It didn't gel.

Past midnight, after the ambulance had taken the body to the local hospital, Kerr and his partner, Don Frazer, drove through the lonely countryside. It was time to face the job for which no constable's salary is enough – breaking the news every parent dreads. Along the way, they heard a radio message that Footscray police had gone to Denis Tanner's house in Melbourne, three hours' drive away, but that he wasn't home.

Kerr knew Denis Tanner was the dead woman's brother-in-law, younger brother of Laurie, the shy farmer and shearer who'd married Jenny a few years before, after his first wife had left him. Denis was a tough detective who'd worked much of his time in Melbourne's inner suburbs; he would soon loom large in Kerr's mind.

But as they turned into the neatly-kept riverside property where Jenny had grown up, the policemen decided to keep any twinges of doubt to themselves. In a few hours, a fatal shooting had become just another sad domestic incident, to be settled as tactfully as possible.

And, despite an inquest twelve months later, that's the way it stayed for eleven years.

The second part of the story starts high on a granite-scarred ridge in the windswept hills of Bonnie Doon in the high country of north-eastern Victoria. On a winter afternoon in 1995, two young men with a long rope, a torch and strong nerves lower themselves into an old mineshaft known only to a few locals and shooters.

The two mates find more than they bargain for: a human skeleton, clothed in faded and rotting feminine things. Next day, a homicide crew arrives with forensic experts and the police search and rescue team, equipped with a tripod, pulleys, ropes and harnesses. Among the bones and remnants of clothes they find a metal bracelet, a boot heel, a wristwatch, a ring, a cigarette lighter, a pocket mirror, a knife, keys, lead shot, a .22 cartridge case and shotgun wads.

But the most interesting and unexpected find is a pair of silicone breast implants that have met their manufacturer's claims by standing up to age, gravity and the elements. And it is these that lead later, with some luck, good detective work and a trip to New Zealand, to identifying the skeleton as the remains of Adele Bailey, a transsexual prostitute who had vanished from St Kilda 17 years before, in the spring of 1978.

Fate deals a card here. By chance, one of the detectives sent to the mineshaft knows the district and some of the people in it. In fact, he knew someone who used to live in a farmhouse in the valley below the ridge.

It is the house where his first cousin, a farmer's wife called Jennifer Tanner, was shot dead 11 years earlier, a death he knows her parents and friends never accepted as suicide, despite a puzzling insistence by police that it was, unlikely as that seemed to those who knew her.

Two violent deaths in a sleepy country district that hadn't seen much crime since the Kelly Gang shot three policemen at Stringybark Creek more than a century before. The coincidence gnaws at the detective and some of his colleagues. They don't believe the two deaths are connected in the sense that one caused another – but they can't help suspecting that whoever had the local knowledge to put the body in the mineshaft might also have had the nerve to kill Jenny Tanner, and set it up to look like a suicide.

The public doesn't know it yet, but there are rumours and rumblings inside the police force, and speculation of an inside investigation of one of their own – Jenny Tanner's brother-in-law, Denis Tanner, a detective sergeant who'd grown up on the old family property near the mineshaft. Already under suspicion by senior officers over unproven allegations that he 'sold out' a drug investigation, Tanner had other interesting parts in his past. He was stationed at St Kilda in 1978, the year Adele Bailey disappeared. The circumstantial evidence about the two deaths has the tang of corruption, cronyism and cover-up, but there is little forensic or eyewitness evidence to back it up.

Two months after the mineshaft gives up its grisly secret, there is another 'coincidence'. The old Tanner homestead, 'Springfield', burns to the ground late on a cool September night, destroying any chance of forensic examination.

The empty house, sold by Denis Tanner's brother (Jennifer's husband Laurie) soon after her death, has an absentee owner who is overseas at the time of the fire. There are no gas or electric appliances being used in the house, which cuts out the most common cause of house fires. And the fire is unusually hot, as if fuelled with paper or other combustibles. It starts inside and burns so fiercely it destroys the building before the local Country Fire Authority brigade gets there.

It is the beginning of a chain of events that leads – after a slow start, and probing of the mystery by a Sunday newspaper – to an exhaustive police investigation, the quashing of the original inquest into Jennifer Tanner's death, and a new inquiry by Victoria's State Coroner, Graeme Johnstone.

The new inquest starts in early October, 1997, and runs for 23 sitting days scattered over more than a year. It is the system's chance to set the record straight for Jennifer Tanner's family and friends. In December 1998, the Coroner brings down his finding.

Sergeant Denis Tanner, he tells a packed court room, killed his sister-in-law, shooting her at least three times, and probably four or more, with her husband's bolt-action .22 rifle.

It was 14 years since Jenny Tanner's body had been found slumped on a couch with the rifle propped between her legs — and 13 years since an inquest hamstrung by the sloppiness of the original police investigation, and haunted by persistent suggestions of a cover-up reaching high into the police force. For the dead woman's blood relatives, justice has not only been agonisingly slow. It seems to them that, for too many painful years, it was denied.

Coroner Johnstone's finding was a damning indictment both of Denis Tanner and the 1985 police investigation.

But despite the public outrage about the case – and the notoriety of the surly, silent man at its centre – one fact had been obvious to police and lawyers from the start:

much of the evidence weighed by the Coroner would be inadmissible in a criminal trial, and therefore it would be no use charging Tanner with murder because there was no chance of a conviction.

Without forensic proof or eye witnesses, the web of circumstantial evidence was not enough to put before a jury. In essence, all Tanner's highly-skilled defence counsel, Joe Gullaci, would have to do is shrug and say that while his client hadn't been particularly fond of his sister-in-law, there was no law against that. And that his instructions were that his client hadn't been anywhere near Bonnie Doon on the night she died. There was no known witness to testify otherwise. Case closed.

Based on the evidence allowed before the court, a judge would be forced to agree, and instruct a jury accordingly.

The result was a faintly bizarre legal stalemate. A bewildered public, having seen and heard headlines saying the Coroner had named Tanner as a killer, could not understand why nothing was being done. The consensus among those outside legal, police and media circles was that someone had 'got away with it'. This sense of outrage was aggravated by the fact that Tanner stayed on the police payroll, a situation that could only change if he resigned – or if the department found a way to dismiss him.

Meanwhile, in early 1999, there was another inquest –

the one into the death of the transsexual Adele Bailey. The State Coroner, Graeme Johnstone, properly ensured there be no suggestion of prejudice by standing down so that another coroner, Jacinta Heffey, would run the inquiry.

Compared with the Jennifer Tanner inquest, it was a relatively quick affair, although not without interest to an onlooker. The search for truth about what happened to a New Zealand-born Pitcairn Islander who had a sex change operation in Cairo before returning to St Kilda to work as a prostitute was bound to attract some interesting witnesses. It did, but in the end it proved only that some very colourful people had managed to survive a quarter century of sex, drugs, crime and law enforcement by failing to recall, at least in the witness stand, details of those incidents that might get other people charged.

Common sense says that Adele Bailey was deliberately abducted and killed. Or that she died in a way that would acutely embarrass a policeman (or policemen) with a sex or drug scandal gone wrong, potentially implicating him (or them) in offences ranging from criminal negligence to corruption to manslaughter.

But there was little chance that street people left over from the 1970s would be supplying the heavy calibre evidence needed for the coroner to make any other finding than the one she swiftly made: an open finding. In the absence of willing and truthful witnesses, no-one can prove how Adele Bailey died, nor how her body came to be in the mineshaft.

The only chance of the truth about Adele Bailey's last hours on earth becoming public is if someone, somewhere, makes a deathbed confession with their last breath. Meanwhile, don't hold yours.

One thing is certain. It won't be Denis Tanner who does the talking. After the Bailey inquest – for which his legal costs were paid by the Police Association, because his connection with Bailey involved his work – he continued his court room policy of silence. Presumably on the same grounds: that is, that to answer questions 'might tend to incriminate' him. As controversy swirled around him for three years he maintained, publicly, a face like a well-kept grave. Even when the State Government specifically amended legislation to give the Chief Commissioner of Police wider powers to dismiss officers – dubbed the 'Tanner clause' – he said nothing publicly.

Instead, poker-faced, he stuck doggedly to his cards and upped the ante. His reputation might have been in tatters, and his family in distress, but he was determined to salvage as much money from the wreckage of his career as he could, in the form of superannuation and leave entitlements. Money, say those who know the man, has always motivated him.

Tanner had an ace up his sleeve when it came to dealing with both police command and with his own union, the Police Association. This was, ironically, his pariah status in the public eye. He was an embarrassment to both sides and, despite any public posture, privately they wanted him to disappear quietly. That gave him the leverage to cut a deal.

It was true that the then Chief Commissioner, Neil Comrie, had the power to sack – but it was also true that the Police Association would be forced to fight such a move because of the wider implications for its members. However, this would be expensive, and it would be unpopular with the public and a lot of police, and erode the political clout the association was building. It was a million-dollar battle neither side really wanted, if face could be saved with some diplomatic manoeuvres.

And another, unspoken, suggestion lingered over the case. Tanner had kept silent not only about himself – but about the possible involvement of other police in various matters that, if revealed, would blow up into scandals calculated to wreck reputations, or worse.

Anybody who had worked 'hot' at inner-suburban police stations such as St Kilda and South Melbourne in the 1970s knew where the bodies were buried, metaphorically speaking. There would be those still in the force, some of them in senior positions, who would be happier for him not to be tempted to remember too much about old times.

A bitter, talkative Tanner with nothing to lose and bent on revenge had the potential to embarrass the entire force as well as, perhaps, ruining several careers. The association knew this as well as senior police did. So there were probably muffled sighs of relief in several quarters when, in July, 1999, he beat a very slow-moving axe by resigning. It was no surprise to find out his representatives had been dickering behind the scenes for some time with police command.

The wisdom of Tanner's policy of stony silence was proven as soon as he opened his mouth. Tanner being deprived of rank and badge meant his public stand-off ended with a whimper rather than a bang.

First, he tried clumsily to quarantine the story of his resignation to two media outlets. This attempt to stare down three years of bad publicity by orchestrating news of his own exit fizzled into farce when heavyweight commercial radio station 3AW neatly scooped him at his own game merely by following up an early-morning 'promo' on Victoria's ABC radio station, plugging his upcoming live appearance with the morning announcer.

Tanner was reduced to choosing the ABC programme in tandem with an obscure publication called the *High*

Country Times, a giveaway local tabloid dropped into the letterboxes of his parents' hometown of Mansfield every Wednesday morning. Its editor and co-proprietor, with whom Tanner had curried favour, happily told 3AW listeners all about the policeman's 'shock' resignation – ten minutes before Tanner himself spoke on ABC radio. This prompted Tanner to complain on air that it was another example of the 'carnivorous' media that, he claimed, had hounded him for three years.

Out of his depth, and struggling under the weight of his own notoriety, Tanner didn't do himself – or the ABC's reputation – any favours.

A distinguishing characteristic of Tanner's progress has been the collateral damage he's inflicted on those around him. It was no different with his resignation.

Tanner offered the radio host the illusion of an 'exclusive', in reality a thinly-veiled, self-serving attempt to manipulate the media. It didn't work well – he sounded nervous, defensive and unconvincing trying to answer the few gentle questions put to him.

Tanner didn't say much, but each word proved the old saying that it's better to shut up and be thought a fool than to speak up and prove it.

He said hesitantly that he had refused to testify at the inquests on the 'best legal advice' of his lawyers. On the question of his guilt he said cautiously: 'Everybody's entitled to an opinion. So be it.' He claimed he had 'plenty' of friends and supporters, but said 'the general public got its mind made up from a media campaign. I can't help it now. It's been done.'

In short, his 'answers' were the farrago of vague generalities, omissions, half truths and specific truths that unreliable witnesses almost always use. The host thanked the disgraced detective and accused killer for talking on the programme. He even offered the self-congratulatory rider that this was because 'we' (the ABC) handled such stories more fairly than others. What he didn't know then, of course, was that he was second choice in a field of two.

The truth was, Tanner had offered his 'exclusive' to senior *Herald Sun* reporter, Geoff Wilkinson, some weeks before… on condition the reporter reveal who'd given his newspaper a copy of Tanner's wedding photograph a few days earlier. Wilkinson refused point blank, forcing Tanner look for a softer target, which he found at the ABC.

The moral is that if you play with snakes, you get bitten. Of course, plenty of other people have come to grief because of Denis Tanner, including his own family. Anybody who saw the inquests unfold over almost two years felt the power of one to cause pain for many.

It's a long way from a dusty church hall in Mansfield in

1985 to the new Melbourne Coroner's Court in 1997. The main players in the drama were the same, if older, but there were a few new faces.

Some were witnesses who probably should have been called in 1985. Others could shed light on certain events since then. Then there were the watchers, drawn to the latest episode of a tragedy that has changed many lives.

Those who attended the inquest, instinctively divided themselves. This subtle segregation was curiously one-sided.

Both (the deceased) Jennifer Tanner and her husband, Laurence James Tanner, belonged to large families.

Jennifer was the eldest of four daughters of Les and Kath Blake, who have lived in the Mansfield district for 30 years, moving there when Jenny was ten.

Laurie Tanner is the oldest of four sons and one daughter of Fred and June Tanner. Tanners have farmed in the district for generations.

For most of the hearing days the Blakes were accompanied by their surviving daughters, Kris, Clare and Miriam. For the first eight days Les Blake's two sisters, Val and Joy, also attended. All except two had to travel from the country and stay in Melbourne at their own expense; none wanted to miss a word of evidence.

The Blakes and their relatives and friends crowded into the right side of the chamber, behind the counsel assisting the coroner, Jeremy Rapke, and the senior task force members given the job of gathering evidence on Jenny Tanner's death.

By contrast, the other side of the room was deserted. Although Laurie Tanner was one of five children of parents who were then still alive, and although he was secretary of the Mansfield agricultural society at the time his wife was killed, no-one came with him and his brother, Denis, then still a detective sergeant in the Victorian police force.

Unlike the Blakes and their relatives and friends, the extended Tanner family evidently did not feel compelled to hear evidence about what might really have happened in the old farmhouse on the night of 14 November, 1984. Denis Tanner told the author 'as far as I am concerned it was a thorough investigation' and that he was satisfied with the assumption Jennifer's death was suicide. Beyond that he would say nothing.

On the second and last day of the inquest a policewoman sat behind Denis Tanner and spoke to him. The only other person to sit voluntarily near the Tanner brothers, and speaking with them, was a retired nurse wanting to write a book about the case.

Denis Tanner, formally named as 'a person of interest' in

the proceedings, retained Gullaci, then a criminal barrister (later a judge) reputed to charge fees in keeping with a reputation that prompted one policeman outside the court to describe him 'as the best advocate going around.'

Such admiration of Gullaci's pugnacious cross-examination won him regular work representing police brought before the courts, in between representing alleged organised crime figures who can afford the best. Interestingly, he also represented Denis Tanner at the first inquest into his sister in-law's death, in 1985.

The 13 years between inquests evidently did not ease Laurie Tanner's concerns. Whereas he shared Gullaci's services with his younger brother in 1985, this time he retained a barrister called Tony Hargreaves, an advocate the Police Association recommends to members in trouble.

Gullaci is short, thickset, bald, with a heavy beard, swarthy looks, a gravel voice and a robust turn of phrase that could earn him a bit part in a mafia movie.

His learned friend, Hargreaves, is taller, younger and less forbidding – more private school than private eye but street smart. The pair worked closely together, arriving early at court each day in a sleek, late model Jaguar with the Tanner brothers in the back seat, taking the most expensive limousine ride of their lives.

At the other end of the horseshoe-shaped bar table,

bristling with nine black microphones, was Jeremy Rapke, the counsel assisting the Coroner. He was a courteous and formal prosecutor whose gentle air masks a steely logic that rattles more than one experienced witness neatly trapped into contradicting their own evidence. The Tanner brothers sat close together, heightening the contrast between them.

Laurie, then about 50, was tall, thin, wrinkled and worried-looking, with curling hair and a droopy moustache under a long, aquiline nose supporting a pair of metal-rimmed glasses. Every day he wore the same grey pinstriped suit. A farmer, truck driver and onetime shearer, he looked uncomfortable in business clothes. Long, bony wrists and calloused hands stuck out a long way from his cuffs, and for days he fidgeted continually, looking vaguely into space, rubbing his fingers together or stroking his chin in a nervous mannerism verging on the compulsive. At the time he had not married again since Jennifer's death, and was living with his parents and motherless son in Mansfield. It was not hard to see why.

The only resemblance between the oldest and the youngest of the Tanners is the hawk-like nose. Where Laurie was scrawny and weathered, worn with manual work, Denis is beefy and broad-shouldered, with the hard look and soft hands of the pub bouncer he has been in the past, a strong man carrying enough weight to give the impression he'd rather risk a little physical danger than lots of physical labour of the sort his brother Laurie did daily.

Despite suggestions raised in court that he had the motive and the opportunity to kill his sister-in-law, the big detective in the well-tailored navy suit sat quietly, his close-set eyes and stony face for the most part elaborately neutral – as if he were a bored bystander, not someone spending tens of thousands of dollars in legal fees to defend his reputation and his career. He rarely moved except to make notes, looked coolest when the evidence seemed most damaging.

From the outset the Coroner, Graeme Johnstone, made it clear it was his investigation, run his way. He was patient, measured, polite, but unflinching. He didn't indulge in the clubby legal humour that often flows between bench and bar table in other courts.

He quietly interrupted testimony and cross-examination with shrewd questions aimed at baring facts hidden by legal persiflage, or by the nervousness or reluctance of witnesses. He was quick to probe examples of the disgraceful police work that clearly frustrated Hugh Adams, the Coroner at the first inquest in 1985, who wouldn't buy the suicide scenario and made an open finding after criticising an investigation he found was 'slanted towards a situation of self-inflicted injuries.'

Jeremy Rapke's opening address flagged some of the drama ahead. For the first time, Sergeant Helen Golding's name was made public. This could have proved a good thing for Sergeant Golding, godmother to Denis Tanner's children, and formerly his wife's best friend, but unlikely to be on speaking terms with the Tanners again.

Rapke revealed that Sergeant Golding had received a series of death threats, but this dramatic revelation paled beside the appearance of the woman herself a week later, an event marked by everyone entering court being checked for weapons by armed police equipped with metal detecting wands.

Visibly shaken, but determined, Sergeant Golding told the court she contacted the task force after reading an account of Jenny Tanner's death in a Sunday newspaper in June, 1996. She said she was 'terrified', and had not slept properly, walked her dog or ridden her horse since making a statement to investigators about Denis Tanner.

Her story was chilling, even in a warm courtroom full of polite people. She was sent a dagger, covered in fake blood, leaflets from funeral directors thanking her for inquiries that she had not made, a sympathy card with the words 'you're dead' written on it, and a .22 calibre bullet in an envelope. What worried her most, perhaps more than the dagger, was a wreath left on her doorstep with the message

'Time runs out'. There was something more sinister in the symbolism of that, somehow, than in the cruder threats of bullets and fake blood.

In July, 1997, she received a letter containing her current work roster, a card with the words 'I miss you' and a letter that read: 'Helen, Are you ignoring the warnings you have received. Do you think they are idle — not so. You're (sic) movements are known – as you can see by the attached roster and you have a new car. How nice. Do not follow through with this – "Life" is not worth it and it won't be worth it. You should have the message by now and if not you soon will. That prick in Melbourne, f...... c... that he is, will soon get his too. If this goes ahead "Your Dead" but not without pain, or alone. You won't get another warning, the moment you make a move to Melbourne start watching your back. Nobody wants to do you any harm but everyone has there (sic) limits and you have pushed yours far enough.'

This campaign of terror prompted an extraordinary statement by the Coroner. After leaving the bench for half an hour, he halted cross-examination to say that although he had sat on many inquests, 'at no stage has a witness been subject to the number of threats as in this.' He said he was troubled by the 'serious nature' of the threats, and called on 'the highest level' of Victoria Police command to guarantee security of Sergeant Golding and her family.

Sergeant Golding's brave evidence was a dramatic postscript to the mystery. But that of the former policeman Bill Kerr went to its heart.

Kerr, an amiable man who plays bowls and wryly called himself 'a dumb country cop', has quietly believed Jennifer Tanner was murdered since an autopsy two days after her death showed she had two bullets in her skull, and bullet wounds in each hand.

Ironically, it was Kerr, called first to the death scene with another policeman, Don Frazer, who began the chain of events that let the death be treated as suicide by others. When he telephoned the nearest Criminal Investigation Branch, at Alexandra, on the night of Jennifer Tanner's death he told (the late) Detective Sergeant Ian Welch the scene 'looked like' a suicide. Welch said not to bother about photographs, forensic tests, or fingerprinting.

Kerr stated he called Welch a second time because he grew suspicious after finding a second empty rifle shell at the scene. Welch doggedly denied this, although his memory failed him on several other points when he was cross-examined. Patchy memories were to affect several witnesses, particularly ex-police.

Kerr spent hours in the stand under withering cross-examination calculated to discredit him, and although he was often tripped up on details of what happened that night, one thing survived his ordeal by lawyer: proof of his suspicion that Jennifer Tanner was murdered.

He said he was puzzled that two hours after the body was found, he heard a police radio message saying attempts to contact Denis Tanner at his (then) Melbourne home had failed. (Golding later gave evidence that Tanner's wife Lynne told her that Denis did not get home until 5am on the night of Jenny Tanner's death.)

Kerr said he was frustrated by 'superiors', who repeatedly denied his requests for forensic tests on the rifle, which he insisted on keeping in his locker at Mansfield police station. His request for a list of questions to be put to Denis Tanner by senior police was also denied.

Months later, Denis Tanner had made a statement to a homicide detective, (the late) Senior Sergeant Albert 'Jimmy' Fry, in which he gave a different alibi from the one he'd given Kerr the day after the shooting. But it was not a record of interview, he was not cautioned, and no meaningful questions were put to him.

Fry, by this time also retired, was called to explain this to the Coroner. A dapper, friendly man with a suntan, slip-on shoes, a big dress ring, and a good line in jokes outside court, Fry could pass for a Sydney car salesman. Questioned by Rapke, he rapidly lost his sense of fun.

He at first claimed it wasn't his 'function' to judge

whether the shooting should be investigated as a possible murder, and that in any case there was not enough information to form an opinion. But, a few minutes later, he admitted writing a seven-point statement that strongly supported the suicide theory and that dismissed Kerr's request that Denis Tanner be questioned, on grounds that Kerr's suggested questions were 'based on rumour and conjecture.' Fry also swore on oath he hardly knew Denis Tanner at the time, and had not spoken to him since, but he admitted calling Tanner in 1996 to urge him to sue *The Sunday Age* because he thought an article (by this author) published about Jenny Tanner's death was 'unfair'.

Fry said he couldn't explain why he didn't realise, after reading the file provided by Kerr, that Tanner had contradicted his original alibi that he was 'at the trots' on the night of the murder. In the statement Tanner made to Fry, he stated he was providing security at a bingo night at Middle Park.

Superintendent Peter Fleming, later of the anti-corruption unit, was assisting the coroner in 1985. He looks like a bank manager who could be trusted not to cook the books. His memory seemed much sharper than that of some other witnesses, particularly Fry and Welch.

Fleming testified bluntly that the investigation of Jenny Tanner's death was 'grossly inadequate' at every level, and that he was concerned that nothing was done to correct it. He recalled an angry meeting at the homicide offices where, he said, Fry 'was adamant it was suicide,' refused to investigate it, and was supported by his superiors.

Fleming said he had also approached the internal investigations division, but was told the matter was beyond its jurisdiction. He had then done the best he could, in limited time, to investigate it himself, despite being warned it wasn't his job.

'There were rumours this particular matter was not being handled correctly,' he said carefully, adding that a decision was made to start the 1985 inquest because of the long delay already endured.

There were several poignant moments in the first week of the hearing. Bill Kerr, asked why he had made and kept tape recordings of conversations with several key people, and why he had taken his file on the case when he retired in 1993, said:

'Because I probably didn't trust them.'

Coroner: 'Why did you answer like that?'

Kerr: 'When I joined the police force in 1970, it had a squeaky clean reputation. I don't believe it has now. That's probably one of the reasons I got out.'

After giving his evidence Frazer, by now a sergeant,

quietly told the Coroner he regretted the way things were handled on the night Jenny Tanner was shot, and volunteered a defence of Kerr's role in having the case re-opened.

'I know the media has jumped on Bill Kerr's comment that he was just "a dumb country cop," but he was far from that, Your Worship. I just wish I'd given him more support — as perhaps others should have,' he said.

Ian Welch, the former detective sergeant who became a carpet cleaner, was asked after a bruising exchange with Rapke how he later thought the case should have been handled.

'The scene should have been preserved, and there should have been a full and proper homicide investigation,' he muttered after an awkward pause. Asked which people a homicide investigation should have interviewed, he said: 'I believe Denis Tanner should have been interviewed.'

'Anybody else?' asked Rapke softly.

'No-one else springs to mind,' replied Welch.

Blood's thicker than water. That's one reason it's so hard to wash away, a point Bruce Tanner could have pondered on a morning in mid-November, 1984, when he drove to the old farmhouse where he'd grown up, to do something so unpleasant he still resents talking about it.

THE SUICIDE THAT WASN'T

The job was this: to scrub blood from the couch where his sister-in-law, Jennifer Tanner, had been found shot dead the night before in circumstances that have come back to haunt the family these past years.

It is unclear exactly why the then school principal interrupted his rushed trip — from Girgarre, near Kyabram, to his parents' house at Mansfield — to spend time cleaning the scene of his sister-in-law's alleged suicide. It's also unclear why two of his brothers, then both policemen, did not later comment on his destroying a possible crime scene. All of which is, or was, a touchy subject with Bruce, judging by his performance in the witness box at the second inquest into Jennifer Tanner's death.

Bruce Frederick Tanner was one of four family members unexpectedly subpoenaed to testify in December 1997. The others were his brother Frank, sister-in-law Lynne and mother June, all called from the country at short notice.

None seemed to enjoy the experience any more than the sorry collection of present and past police facing the humiliation of admitting their parts in a 1984 'investigation' they insist was merely 'inept', but over which lingers the whiff of cover-up, cronyism, collusion and corruption. The death scene was not secured, photographs were not taken, forensic tests not done, and a pathologist's suspicions were dismissed. From the first hour the death was treated as a suicide, for reasons which clearly perplexed the coroner, whose task was to unravel the mystery of how she died — if she didn't commit suicide, as seemed painfully obvious. It's a mystery that drew a lot of people to court, many of them blood relatives of Jennifer's there to support her parents.

They watched, with the awful fascination of onlookers at a car crash, the spectacle of the Tanner family being torn apart.

Mostly, the Tanners were notable by their absence, except for the pair deemed 'persons of interest', the brothers Laurie and Denis. But when his family was called, Laurie wasn't in court. His banister handed a doctor's certificate to the coroner to explain his client that was too ill to attend.

He stressed the certificate was 'confidential', but promptly revealed its thrust: that the visibly nervous Laurie was distressed by intense media coverage of the case. The coroner ordered that the Tanner brothers not be filmed or photographed outside the court until they were actually called as witnesses.

This order, however, did not extend to the rest of the family, which was to lead to an extraordinary scene outside court, which happened after four Tanners had given evidence.

Bruce Tanner cut a neat figure in a conservative dark suit, metal-rimmed glasses and moustache. The second of the Tanner brothers could have passed for a solicitor, accountant or businessman. That is, until he answered the first question put by Jeremy Rapke, counsel assisting the coroner.

The quietly-spoken Rapke, whose courtesy a witness should not mistake for weakness, asked Bruce Tanner his occupation. 'Depends what time of year you're talking about,' came the tart retort. 'Currently I'm a company director.'

The exchange set the tone for the next half hour. Swallowing hard, but defiant, Tanner gritted his way through cross-examination about the intriguing events of the day after Jennifer's death.

His version of those events was that his mother telephoned him about 6am on 15 November, 1984, with bad news: his older brother Laurie had returned home from Mansfield the night before to find his wife dead on the couch with his .22 rifle between her knees.

After arranging for staff to fill in for him at his school, Bruce set out for Mansfield to comfort his parents and Laurie. But instead of driving past the farmhouse, which is next to the highway at Bonnie Doon, he stopped and went in.

Asked why he did this instead of going straight to his grieving relatives, Tanner retorted: 'Because the police had informed my mother she was expected to clean up, and there was no way she was going to do that.' Unfortunately, he didn't know the answer to a crucial question: which policeman allegedly gave his mother this peculiar direction.

Asked how he cleaned the blood from the sofa, he snapped, 'How do you usually clean blood off?'

Rapke: 'I don't know, Mr Tanner. Tell me.'

Tanner: 'Cold water. That's what you use to clean blood off.'

Asked why he hadn't inquired about the circumstances surrounding the death, he said he had gone overseas a few weeks later, and hadn't returned for more than a year.

He conceded 'probably' discussing Jennifer's death with his brother, Denis, but said he didn't know two bullets had been found in Jennifer's skull until after he returned from overseas. He also claimed not to have known she had bullet wounds in both hands until he 'read it in the papers' during the current investigation.

'You read all this crap in the papers. Who knows if it's true?' he snapped, scowling.

Rapke: 'Do you resent being here?'

Tanner: 'I'm losing a day's pay. I have been unemployed for seven months. I just got a job and just when I start I am being dragged here.'

But fears for his reputation didn't curb his temper after that day's hearing. Nor brother Denis's. At a time when it might be prudent not to show a propensity for violence, the two Tanner brothers blew it.

As the family group walked to the court car park, one brother hit a *Herald Sun* photographer in the groin with a brief case. Then the other threw open his car door as he accelerated away, knocking the same photographer to the ground. In the car, Denis's wife Lynne, a former policewoman, looked as shattered as she'd looked in court a few hours earlier...

Lynne Maree Tanner was a police officer for 12 years, and must have seen plenty of courts, but the blonde, pleasant-looking mother of four looked as bewildered in the witness box as any first timer.

Her voice was faint, and quavered. If she expected a tough time from Rapke, she was right. He fired questions like punches aimed at a sore spot: the fact her husband Denis had given two alibis for where he was on the night of Jennifer's death. One, that he was 'at the trots' was demonstrably false. Which might be why he came up with another, that he was doing security at a bingo hall in

Middle Park, which was vague and hard to substantiate.

She said Denis told her he was going to the bingo, but can't recall what night it was, when he left or when he got home to their house in Spotswood. In a curiously roundabout answer, she said she doesn't remember him arriving, but that she 'would have remembered' if he hadn't been home when she got up to feed their baby at 1am.

She shook when Rapke refers to the covert police recording of conversations she had with the godmother of her children, Sergeant Helen Golding. She sobbed when reminded that Golding, her closest friend for years, has given evidence that Lynne told her privately Denis arrived home on the night of the shooting just before Footscray police came to the door around 5am.

The court adjourned for 15 minutes while the distressed woman rushed out in tears, to be comforted in the women's toilets by her mother-in-law, the flint-faced June Tanner. Meanwhile, her husband stayed in court, chewing gum and chatting nonchalantly to his barrister, who didn't look happy.

After her return, Rapke resumed the attack: 'Helen Golding told this court you told her he (Denis) came home just before the police called.'

Lynne Tanner: 'I don't recall saying it... to my knowledge he was home.'

THE SUICIDE THAT WASN'T

There were many other questions, some put by the Coroner. At face value, the answers revealed a woman with astonishingly little knowledge of either her husband of 15 years or of her sister-in-law's death.

No, she didn't know Denis belonged to a pistol club, and couldn't recall him criticising Jennifer the way some other people did. No, she didn't take any interest in the evidence at the first inquest, in 1985. No, she didn't know there were two bullets in Jennifer's skull until the first inquest, and that fact didn't arouse her curiosity or suspicions. No, she didn't know about the bullet holes in the hands 'until the last couple of years.'

She said she had never heard rumours of her husband's possible involvement in the shooting. And she didn't know if Denis had driven to Bonnie Doon a few weeks before Jennifer's death to warn her to 'treat Laurie properly.'

Frank Tanner and his mother, June, got their turn in the box three days later. Frank, who gave his occupation as farm hand, had his sleeves rolled up and chewed gum as he gave evidence. Not as volatile as Bruce, not as nervous as Lynne, he was offhand and taciturn.

He told the court that when Jennifer was killed he was a police constable at Hamilton. That 'as far as I know' Laurie and Jennifer were happily married. That it never crossed his mind 'other things' but suicide might have caused

Jennifer's death, that he had 'nothing to do with Denis,' and had never discussed the case with him.

'I had no idea until the publicity recently that she was shot twice,' he said, which prompted the Coroner to quiz him from the bench, a touch sceptically.

Coroner: 'But Jennifer Tanner is family, is she not? And you didn't inquire as to why it was an open finding (in 1985). You would be more aware than most (as a policeman) about the meaning of an open finding. And that finding was critical of the investigation.'

Frank Tanner: 'What's it to do with me?'

Coroner: 'Did you seek out your brother and ask what was happening?'

Frank Tanner: 'No.'

Coroner: 'You are disinterested?'

He hesitated, then answered slowly: 'Oh, I've thought about it a bit the past 12 or 18 months or so. I don't talk to my family about it.'

He confirmed he accompanied Laurie to inspect Jennifer's skull at the Mansfield undertaker's after the body was exhumed in the previous year, July 1996. But he said he no longer reads the papers or watched television news, and didn't discuss 'certain things' with his family.

Coroner: 'Tell me, Mr Tanner. Does this current

investigation raise doubts in your mind as to the way Jennifer died?'

Tanner: 'It probably has. I still believe she committed suicide – but obviously I would be a fool if I didn't think about it.'

He'd been 'a bit sad' when the Springfield farmhouse mysteriously burned to the ground in late 1995, after the discovery of Adele Bailey's skeleton in the mineshaft that the Tanner brothers knew well as children growing up in the district.

He said he assumed the house burned because of 'an electrical fault.' This despite evidence given earlier that a car and a person had been seen near the house when the fire started.

He said he had been 'out fencing' when he'd got a call 18 months before from Laurie to say there was going to be 'an article in the paper on the Sunday.'

'I think he (Laurie) might have been a bit upset that they were going to point the bone at him.'

Rapke: 'Has the bone been pointed at any other brother?'

Tanner (laughing): 'I think so, don't you? It's been pointed at Denis.'

Rapke: 'You can't believe that any member of your family could stoop to murder?'

Tanner: 'I wouldn't think they could; anyone that takes a mother away from her little baby is pretty ordinary.'

June Tanner, then a thin woman in her 70s, gave her sons the characteristic aquiline nose and a hardy attitude. She dropped her tan handbag on the seat provided in the witness box and stood, ready for action.

Questioned by Rapke, she fiercely denied that Denis ever had a share of the family farm, Springfield, which Laurie had taken over when he married his first wife, Suzanne, in the early 1970s.

She said she knew nothing of the divorce settlement Laurie reached with Suzanne. Other evidence had been led that Laurie Tanner paid $20,000 to Suzanne when she left him, and that Denis later told a Benalla motel broker that he (Denis) had made sure 'the second slut' wouldn't get the lot. But June Tanner would have none of it. She said she knew nothing of Laurie agreeing to join Denis in a motel venture in the late 1980s. She said none of her sons had any interest in guns, and that she was sure Denis was never a member of a pistol club.

She said she 'got on very well with Jenny, as a matter of fact' and 'popped in and saw her a lot,' but that she knew nothing about the state of Jennifer and Laurie's marriage.

She said Jennifer was 'very moody' but she didn't know whether she was contemplating leaving Laurie. She snapped 'I wouldn't have a clue' three times in answer to questions about Jennifer's avowed dislike of guns.

Rapke: 'Are you close to your sons?'

June Tanner: 'Yes, we are a normal happy family.'

A few seconds later, she added: 'It's 13 years. It's a long time. A lot of people have got exalted ideas about what happened.'

She denied cleaning the house, and didn't give a direct answer when asked if any policeman had told her to clean it. 'That Bill Kerr, I don't know what he told anybody,' she said darkly – and meaninglessly.

Asked if she had any suspicions about the death, she said: 'I am not interested. I'm just interested in bringing my grandson up. You just have to get on with life.

'If it was murder, that would be shocking. I don't follow these things. I don't read the papers.' But a few seconds later, asked how and when she learned Jennifer had two bullet wounds to the head, she answered: 'It was in the paper.'

As she leaves the witness box she snapped, 'Excuse me!' at an investigator as she stepped over his feet. Then she smiled across the room at Denis. He smiled back.

Much more evidence was given over eight days. It divided into two broad categories: police and former police attempting to explain their actions during what is loosely termed 'the first investigation', and expert witnesses demonstrating how unlikely it was that Jennifer Tanner shot herself. The testimony of Dr Norman Sonenberg comes in between.

Sonenberg had the misfortune to help the late Dr Peter Dyte perform an autopsy on Jennifer Tanner's body two days after her death. Because Dyte was terminally ill at the time of the first inquest (later quashed) in 1985, Sonenberg was obliged to give evidence on which he had to be re-examined.

It wasn't pleasant for him. Faced with expert opinion from a professor of neurosurgery and a professor of pathology, he elected to fall on his scalpel. He admitted he and Dyte — a polite and deferential man — tried in 1984 to make the two head wounds and two hand wounds fit the police's dogged insistence that it was a suicide. Sonenberg admitted his evidence at the 1985 inquest was unreliable, as was a statement to police last year. 'We were trying to make a round peg fit a square hole,' he said. 'We were trying to make the wounds and the scenario fit a suicide. We spent some time trying to make it fit.'

Sonenberg blamed police for dismissing any possibility of suicide. He didn't name Neil Phipps, then a sergeant at Mansfield, but the since-retired policeman himself admitted being wrong.

Phipps, later a chief inspector, and a former homicide detective, told the inquest he'd suddenly changed his mind. He no longer believed Jennifer Tanner could have twice shot herself in the skull.

'What I am saying is that there is a strong possibility that the firearm was operated by someone other than Jennifer Tanner,' he admitted in the witness stand.

Evidence was given earlier by Bill Kerr, the more senior of the two police called to the scene, that Phipps did not attend that night because he was 'working a phantom' night shift, and wasn't at the police station when the first call came.

An uncomfortable Phipps denied working the 'phantom' shift, but said he 'blanked out' some details about the case after transferring from Mansfield a few days after Jennifer Tanner's death.

Duncan MacLennan was another former policeman with a problem. MacLennan, who in 1984 was the district inspector, admitted there was a 'general consensus' around the station a few days after the shooting that Denis Tanner might have been involved. He said he couldn't explain Kerr's clear evidence that his brief to the first inquest has been doctored to remove material implicating Tanner.

MacLennan was caught. He could choose to praise Kerr as a diligent and honest senior constable, thus drawing criticism because Kerr's recommendations that Denis Tanner be questioned were ignored. Or he could try to dismiss Kerr as an eccentric dreamer with little experience, as some others tried to do, leaving himself open to the accusation he left a possible or likely murder in the hands of someone clearly incapable of investigating it.

In the event, he chose to praise Kerr. And to make the lame claim it wasn't his responsibility to supervise the investigation 'because I was an administrator, not an investigator'.

Pushed by the Coroner to explain why it wasn't a cover-up, he first said it was 'obviously a case of inept police work'. But, asked to explain why Kerr's statement was edited before reaching the Coroner in 1985, he changed tune. 'It implies a cover-up or attempted cover-up. It is not acceptable.'

The Coroner asked if the death was not properly investigated because a serving policeman was involved. MacLennan replied: 'As far as I am concerned, Your Worship, no. I can't speak for others.'

Before the inquest the biggest of many questions facing the Coroner was how Jennifer Tanner could shoot herself twice in the brain and through the hands with a bolt-action rifle. That would have appeared to have been put beyond reasonable doubt: She couldn't and didn't.

Someone else shot her, possibly three or four times. Which left some other unanswered questions.

One was this. Even if the investigation was botched from the start by 'inept' police, why did they keep secret – especially from her parents – for almost a year the fact there were two bullet wounds to both the skull and one in each hand?

There were many other questions – about false alibis, inexplicably poor investigation, cronyism, collusion and intimidation. But one that should have been asked the night Jenny Tanner died still stands out.

How could she shoot herself twice in the head, and through both hands, with a bolt-action rifle that she would have to cock before each shot, yet still be found with one hand curled around the barrel?

CHAPTER 9
FALLING DOWN

'Within seconds of me tossing the parcel I heard a huge bang, which was similar to a huge firecracker being let off in a small space.'

Nobody who knew Colin Dunstan was surprised that he finally flipped out. It was the way he did it that shocked people.

In America, they call it 'going postal' – blackly humorous shorthand for the murderous madness that can make someone take out a gun at work and start shooting until the ammunition runs out and the SWAT team runs in. The 'postal' tag comes from the fact, which has entered urban folklore, that several US mail workers have done such a thing, wreaking revenge for real or imagined grievances of the sort that fester in the souls of little people toiling for giant organisations.

Variations on a theme of being mad as hell and not taking it any more are not new, of course. They have infiltrated popular culture, feeding the revenge fantasies of loopy loners who see themselves as some sort of persecuted suburban heroes – like the out-of-control everyman that

Michael Douglas plays in the film *Falling Down*, which has become a reference point for describing outbursts of extraordinary violence by otherwise ordinary men.

But Canberra is not California and, thankfully, Colin Dunstan wasn't marching to a beat that demanded an AK-47 assault rifle. When the prim and proper public servant 'went postal', he did it literally... he made letter bombs. Not that Dunstan would agree with the 'bomb' word. At his trial, he maintained that while the twenty-eight 'devices' he posted might have resembled realistic letter bombs, they wouldn't actually explode. And, even if they did, they wouldn't hurt anyone. Much, anyway.

The problem with running that defence is that one of the devices had detonated when being handled even before it was opened. And if that hadn't happened in time to warn the authorities, then twenty-six other identical packages would have ended up in the letter boxes of people high on Dunstan's long list of 'enemies'. Any one of them, according to the police and the prosecution, had the potential to injure. And all were calculated to terrify. It's all a long way from trouble around the tea trolley in the Australian Tax Office. But that's where Colin Dunstan's fall began.

Colin George Dunstan's origins are as prosaic and stolid as his name suggests. The middle child – but only son – of five children born to a respectable Wollongong couple in the 1950s, he was by all accounts a conscientious boy who helped his father with his vegetable garden and hobby of breeding birds and small animals.

Young Colin worked hard at school, apparently as a way of gaining his father's praise, which he craved but felt he didn't get, a psychiatrist would later say. The diligent boy grew into a self-absorbed young man who shone in maths and science subjects, finishing in the top fifty science students in New South Wales in his final year.

He left home at eighteen years old to go to the Australian National University in Canberra, where in 1974 he met the woman who was to become his first wife. They married in 1977, the year he took his arts degree, and later had three daughters.

Intelligent and meticulous, Dunstan had 'obsessional traits' that became more pronounced with age – and which, his psychiatrist noted drily in a report tendered in court, were shared by 'most good public servants'.

He later took woodwork, cooking and electronics classes in his own time. A lean man who kept fit and dressed neatly, he was good with his hands as well as his mind, and was attracted early to information technology. He came to be seen as something of a computer expert before a wave of younger, computer-literate staff entered the public service in the 1990s, by which time his star was rapidly dimming.

Dunstan's troubles began when he transferred to the Tax Office from another department in 1987. At age thirty-two, his psychiatrist was to testify later, he wanted a 'fresh challenge'. That is, a fresh challenge by public servant standards.

He didn't want to become a skydiving instructor or trek through the Andes. He didn't even want to do anything that would alter his daily routine of going to work in Canberra's rabbit warren of anonymous offices. All he wanted was to be appointed a Data Base Administrator.

He got the job, but trouble came with the territory. A married woman he had known slightly in 1982 in another department was one of his subordinates. She began, he was to complain later, to plague him for advice about problems. She contrived excuses to see him in person, and made it clear she was infatuated with him.

It was the beginning of a bizarre interlude in which the woman – whose name has been suppressed by court order – allegedly began to stalk Dunstan and his family. Dunstan's wife received mysterious 'hang-up' telephone calls and the woman once confronted her. When Dunstan's psychiatrist later described this period in a report, he put it under the heading Fatal Attraction.

Dunstan became depressed and rattled; it showed in his work and his behaviour. He fell into a short-lived affair with the woman, who had pursued him for four years. This aggravated his problems and was eventually to end his marriage and his career. He became isolated from friends, family and workmates.

In early 1992, he moved out of his family home and into a flat and attempted suicide with an overdose of prescription painkillers. His worried wife, meanwhile, approached the other woman's husband to try to end what she saw as years of harassment.

The already bizarre situation spun out of control and began to involve others when the woman complained to an equal opportunity officer, who allegedly took her side and wrote a letter suggesting that the Dunstans had 'intimidated and harassed' the woman. Dunstan's version of events, as told to his psychiatrist and lawyers, is that the woman orchestrated a revenge campaign against him by making spurious complaints to his superiors and to the Human Rights and Equal Opportunities Commission.

The Tax Office responded by trying to make it go away – transferring both Duncan and the woman to other sections.

Dunstan recovered from his suicide attempt and continued his struggle against the system with renewed bitterness. By then divorced from his wife, he met and married another woman who encouraged his belief that he was a victim. It seemed to him that while the other woman continued to be promoted, his own career had been stalled, if not derailed. In his mind, he'd been made a scapegoat for a mess not of his making, while the real culprit was going unpunished.

And he believed that other people now involved in the dispute had unfairly sided against him, pre-judging his case so that the more he tried to prove his point, the more they opposed him. All of which might have sounded like just another paranoid delusion, but the factual basis of Dunstan's dilemma was not lost on the judge who sifted through the facts. Though nothing excused Dunstan's actions, the judge was to say, it was clear why he had such a grievance against the system. But that was later.

For Nelly Campbell, it was just another nightshift at the Canberra mail centre in Fyshwick, the faintly industrial underbelly of the model modern city.

On 1 December, 1998, a Tuesday evening, the 35-year-old mother started at 6pm sharp, as she usually did, intending to work until exactly 1.51am next morning.

Nelly Campbell and three workmates started the shift by moving a big steel crate of unsorted parcels into what they call the 'bull ring', then sorting them into a series of tubs. At 7.45pm, they switched to 'indexing' – typing postcodes on envelopes so that they could be easily and accurately sorted. At 9.25pm, the crew had a rest break, starting again at 10pm on a new task. At midnight, they started the last job of the night – sorting small parcels. The crew sorted the first crate of parcels in about 15 minutes, then Campbell fetched another bin and they started work.

'We had only been sorting this particular bin for about a minute or two,' she was to recall, 'when I picked up two small white-coloured parcels. I checked the suburb and postcode and tossed the (first) parcel in the Queanbeyan area bin. As soon as I had done this I realised I had mis-sorted the parcel — meaning I had tossed it into the wrong bin. While I still had one of the parcels in my hand I picked up another parcel which looked exactly the same as the one I had tossed and the same as the one I still had in my hand.

'I checked the suburb and postcode and this time leaned so I was closer to the tub and wouldn't mis-sort and tossed the parcel into the tub. Within seconds I heard a huge bang, which was similar to a huge firecracker being let off in a small space. At first, I saw a white light coming from the tub and then I saw smoke. (It) filled the area where I was standing. I could smell what I thought was gunpowder... I felt things hitting me but I didn't realise what they were.

'I looked down and saw a lot of blue plastic pieces. That's

when I realised what had hit me.' Two senior mail officers grabbed the tub and moved it away from the workers.

Nelly Campbell's ears were ringing, one arm felt numb and she was gripped by the shock that was to stop her working for eight months. But she remembered she'd seen more than a dozen parcels identical to the one that had exploded, and said so. They were all about the size of a computer disc, she said, but about two centimetres thick, and wrapped in white paper, with addresses neatly printed. Each had two stamps — a two-dollar blackwood tree stamp and a 30-cent saltwater crocodile stamp.

All neat and tidy, like scones from the same perfect batch.

An acting sergeant in the Federal Police took the call about 3am. By the time he got to the mail centre, the bomb experts and forensic police had secured the scene and started the painstaking job of gathering evidence. Which, in this case, meant more than just using vacuum equipment and tape-lifts to gather explosive propellant residue and broken plastic.

They had to look for letter bombs and disable them. The police worked all night. By seven o'clock that morning, they had 21 identical white parcels and were satisfied there were no more in the mail exchange. But the police knew what the public didn't: that a letter bomb had been detected and defused in Sydney the day before, and that it matched the 20 they now had.

So how many more were there in the postal system? There was no way of knowing how many had been sent, or where, until the offender was found.

The police hit the telephones. The first lead: the return address on each of the suspect parcels had the name 'D. O'DONNELL' and a Canberra street and suburb. Then there were the names and addresses on each of the 21 parcels.

It didn't take long to establish that one Daniel O'Donnell had nothing to do with sending the letter bombs – but there was a connection. His mother was a public servant who'd had dealings with someone known to 21 other potential recipients.

By mid-morning, a flurry of telephone calls, followed with flying visits, had established that they were all linked by one thing. When each was asked if he or she knew anyone who might make and send letter bombs, most nominated Colin Dunstan.

The police converged on Dunstan's house in Palmerston in the early afternoon. First, trained negotiators had telephoned the house to ensure that Dunstan was not holding his wife hostage. He wasn't. Knowing police were on the way, Dunstan's wife, Sokkha Hac, took some computer disks and threw them over her back fence, a court was later told.

The police recovered the disks, but there was no retrievable information left on them. There was, however, other evidence in and around the house that matched grains of gunpowder, pieces of plastic and other material they'd found at the mail exchange.

Now they were sure of their man, but not where he was. One thing was sure: if his wife knew, she wasn't saying.

Police in every state were watching for the Canberra letter bomber. His photograph and description had been circulated nation-wide; every airport was alerted in case he tried to flee the country. But the wanted man was closer to home than anyone imagined.

On the Tuesday morning, more than 12 hours before the furore at the mail centre, a man driving a undistinguished blue Toyota Corona drove into the Curtin Budget Motel, a small motel near a riding school about ten minutes from the city.

He booked in, giving his name to the duty manager as Ron White, and was shown to room six. The motel owner, Les McCabe, was interested to see the name in the ledger because he had worked with a Ron White in Sydney years before, and wondered if it was the same man. McCabe was left wondering that day because the man stayed in his room.

A long-term resident in the next room noticed an odd thing about the quiet man in number six. Each morning that week, 'Ron White' got up when his alarm went at 6am, started his Toyota precisely 15 minutes later and let it idle for quarter of an hour before driving off in the direction of the nearest McDonald's store. In an era when few people bother warming car motors, it seemed an elaborately painstaking routine.

The guest had paid $150 in advance for three nights. On Friday, his last morning, he went to reception and offered $20 to be able to check out late, at noon. The McCabes noticed he still hadn't left when they began their lunch, but they weren't overly concerned. When Les McCabe returned to the office the guest was waiting for him. He was sitting outside the door trying to hide the fact he was holding a blood-soaked wad of paper to one wrist.

McCabe grabbed the paper and had a look. There were two deep cuts in the man's arm. He had obviously lost a lot of blood. McCabe bundled him into the car and drove him to hospital.

Left to cool his heels in the casualty waiting room, McCabe started to sense something odd when he inquired about 'Ron White' with a nurse, and no patient of that name came up on the computer screen. McCabe also noticed that the nurse looked unusually flustered. What he didn't know until later was that she had just called the police because the suicidal patient virtually admitted he was the letter bomber, and had asked for his lawyer to be called. He also said he had taken a drug overdose and would die of liver failure within days.

Still unaware of the drama unfolding around him, McCabe left the mysterious guest to it and drove back to the motel – only to find it surrounded by police cars and news crews. The police blocked his way, and when he identified himself they put him in a car with two detectives who questioned him.

It was then he found out that the guest in room six was Australia's most wanted man. It turned out that while he was at the hospital his wife had gone to clean the room. She found blood in the bathroom and a note on a table saying there were no weapons or bombs in the room and requesting the finder to tell his wife that he'd put money in the bank to pay the mortgage.

Mrs McCabe knew the guest had to be the letter bomber. She called the police, only to be told that she was probably mistaken because they believed Dunstan had fled to Queensland.

Half an hour later, a constable turned up and acknowledged that the blue Toyota looked like Dunstan's car, but had the wrong number plates. But when he found the car's correct plates in a bag in the front seat there was no doubt about it. He had a quick look at room six and locked it to preserve the scene.

When the bomb squad arrived later they started, to the McCabes' disgust, to break down the door instead of asking for the key. The bomb men were disappointed – there was nothing in the room except the note and the bloodstains, and there were traces only of what turned out to be gunpowder in the car. Forensic evidence, maybe, but nothing that would go bang.

On Monday, 7 December, Bob Platt was taking a drive in his lunch hour from a concrete works on the western outskirts of Canberra. He was in Urialla Road, a semi-rural area favoured for picnics, when he saw something sitting underneath a tree close to the road. Curious, he stopped his car and got out.

He found five plastic bags, but they weren't full of rubbish of the sort often dumped in quiet spots. It was a strange collection of hardware: tools, wires and electrical components. There were also hundreds of rifle bullets in various calibres ranging from the common .22 to .243 to .308, and 12-gauge shotgun cartridges. Some of the bullets and cartridges were empty, and there was a bag of bullet heads, lead shot, and wads. It was obvious someone had been extracting gunpowder.

But it wasn't the ammunition that alarmed Bob Platt. It was the small plastic device the size of a computer disk. He'd seen a picture of the devices found at the mail centre seven days before, and this looked awfully like it. He left quickly and quietly.

When the police came they found something else in the bags: a list of names and addresses of people, including the 28 to whom letter bombs had been mailed the previous week.

There were also three two-dollar blackwood stamps and three 30-cent saltwater crocodile stamps. Investigators already had enough forensic evidence to convict Dunstan, but this put it beyond doubt. As long as the link was established with Dunstan, no defence lawyer could dismiss it as scientific mumbo jumbo, and no jury could ignore it.

It would be a year before the scales of justice weighed the evidence against Dunstan, but his fate was sealed that day.

Colin George Dunstan, 44, was found guilty of nine charges relating to mailing 28 explosive devices. He admitted making the devices, but insisted they were not dangerous and that he had taken steps to ensure they wouldn't explode. Judge Higgins, of the ACT Supreme Court, sentenced Dunstan to nine years' jail, with a non-parole period of five years, backdated to the time of arrest.

In his judgment, Judge Higgins noted: 'It seems to

be that the situation was encouraged by the absurdly complicated grievance mechanisms engaged in within the Australian Public Service generally, and the Australian Taxation Office in particular. He was not alone in being responsible for elevating a relatively simple workplace difficulty into an intractable and lengthy series of administrative and legal proceedings.'

But, the judge said, 'whatever wrongs the addressees may have committed, that could not remotely have justified the campaign of terror the offender planned.' Dunstan's actions, he said, were 'a product of self-pity and a desire for revenge' out of all proportion to the actions against him.

CHAPTER 10
THE FINGER OF SUSPICION

Bruce Burrell was good at keeping up appearances.

There's a Raymond Chandler feel to Maroubra. Its sunbaked streets of ageing stucco and tile houses, sprawled next to Coogee on Sydney's eastern beaches, suggest Chandler's between-the-wars Los Angeles. So do some of the goings-on there.

It was here, in a street with a million-dollar view of the Pacific, that a little old lady with a big bank balance went for a walk and never came back.

Chandler himself couldn't have plotted the last-known movements of Mrs Dottie Davis more bleakly, or have left fewer clues. Late on a Tuesday morning in May 1995, the 74-year-old widow came home to her ugly double-storey brick house at 9 Undine Street, after an appointment with her doctor.

About an hour later, according to a builder working on an awning at the back of the house, the old woman said she was going to visit a sick friend. The builder wasn't wearing a watch, and could later offer only vague estimates of crucial times, a fact that was to earn him the undivided attention of detectives who considered him, briefly, the best suspect they had.

What the unfortunate tradesman could tell police was that Mrs Davis did not drive her Mercedes. The signs were that she didn't intend to go far, or to stay long. Though she suffered badly from arthritis, she walked. She left meat out to defrost, and the prescription her doctor had just written was on the kitchen table.

The old lady walked down the drive, past the fake antique gaslight and the rickety letterbox, and was never seen again.

Undine Street is only a dozen houses long and slopes down towards the bay. At the bottom of the street, probably 60 metres from Mrs Davis's house, a walker can turn right into a footpath that skirts the shore in front of a few houses.

The last of these buildings, on the next corner, is a stylish duplex pair. One of the pair, 34 Marine Parade, was in 1995 the home of a close family friend of Mrs Davis. This was Dallas Burrell, who'd known Mrs Davis all her life, and called her 'Auntie Dot'.

In May 1995, Mrs Burrell had just been diagnosed with cancer. Police now consider it highly likely she was the sick friend Mrs Davis intended to visit. As far as they can tell, no one else fitting that description lived within walking distance. In 1995, the Burrell connection was only one of many possibilities for puzzled police. That would change.

When Mrs Davis vanished, police spoke to Dallas Burrell, and to her husband Bruce. It was a routine inquiry. The Burrells, after all, were a respectable professional couple. Dallas Burrell was an advertising art director, and her husband worked for a Sydney advertising agency, Peter Grace and Associates.

Not only was there nothing to link either of the Burrells with the disappearance of a dear family friend but both seemed understandably distressed.

What police didn't know, nor would they have cared then, was that Bruce Burrell had been retrenched five years before by the Australian arm of the international forklift firm, Crown Equipment, which has its national headquarters in Smithfield in Sydney.

Business had been tough for Crown in 1990. The company liked to think of itself as a big family but, when the crunch came, heads had to roll to cut costs. One of them belonged to Bruce Burrell, the advertising manager, until then one of the close-knit management team. He was called into the executive offices on the top floor of the Smithfield address. There, he faced the man who had been chief executive of the company since 1974, and had become its Asia-Pacific vice-president. A man who had known Burrell through work, tennis days and shooting trips for more than ten years, and who thought it his duty to wield the axe personally. His name was Bernie Whelan.

Bruce Burrell was good at keeping up appearances. He always had cash to spend, according to workmates, but privately he was doing it hard. Friends later told police they suspected his wife largely supported him, and that his 'advertising' job was as a contract salesman, a hand-to-mouth existence compared with his days as a high-flying marketing executive.

Coincidentally, after Dorothy Davis's disappearance, the Burrells' marriage broke up. Dallas Burrell moved from the smart duplex at 34 Marine Parade just up the road to number 44, a big block of flats – luxurious by 1960s standards – sitting on a headland overlooking the ocean. Her estranged husband, meanwhile, moved to the 192-hectare property he had bought some years before at Bungonia, near Goulburn, in the southern tablelands.

Burrell's property is the last on a quiet track beyond Bungonia township, which comprises only a dozen houses and no shops. There, according to locals, he lived alone after his marriage breakdown and mostly kept out of people's way. One neighbour would recall Burell 'enjoys a beer and a talk', but not many have had the chance to find out even that much about the bloke from Sydney.

In Goulburn, 30 kilometres away, few remember that Bruce Burrell was once a local. In fact, according to a local optometrist, on at least one occasion Burrell wasn't keen to remember it himself.

It happened some time in 1996, when Mr Burrell stepped into the optometrist's shop. He had glasses, and might have wanted to look at a new pair or have his eyes tested, the proprietor can't remember which. What he does recall is Burrell's reaction when the optometrist remarked that he'd known him as a child because his father, Alan Burrell, had once worked for the family as a wool classer.

To his surprise, Burrell bluntly contradicted him. 'He said, "Oh, no. That's not right",' the optometrist was to recall. Several other people in Goulburn remember Alan 'Splinter' Burrell, who lived at West Goulburn with his family, including a son called Bruce, before moving to Sydney in the 1960s. They have no doubt it is the same Bruce Burrell.

The optometrist had no reason to dwell on this trifling exchange until May this year. That was when the wife of the man who had sacked Bruce Burrell seven years before, vanished without trace.

The facts of Kerry Whelan's last-known movements are few and worn with retelling. But when the 39-year-old mother of three went missing on Tuesday, 6 May, 1997, only her family, close friends and police knew. It was kept secret for the next ten days. Then the media were told, but police negotiated a news blackout for another six days.

So it wasn't until 21 May that the rest of Australia heard the news that had crushed Bernie Whelan and his children, Sarah, 15, Mathew, 13, and James, 11.

After breakfast on 6 May, Kerry Whelan drove her new silver Land Rover Discovery from the family's lush property at Kurrajong, in the foothills of the Blue Mountains, to Parramatta, where it was due for its first service. And where, she had told her family, she was to have a beauty treatment before accompanying her husband to Adelaide on a business trip that afternoon.

The secretary who'd married her much-older boss after an office romance 16 years before, retained a business-like habit of keeping a meticulous daily appointment diary. But for that Tuesday she had made only one cryptic entry: 'Parramatta 9.30.'

She had been running late. The security film recovered from the car park underneath the Parkroyal Hotel in Parramatta shows that she drove in at 9.36am.

After speaking to attendants at the boom gate, she parked near the entrance. Leaving the keys in the ignition so an attendant could later move it to another spot, she took her bag and walked quickly out to the street, as if late for something. She hasn't been seen since.

When she didn't meet her husband at 3.45pm, ready for the Adelaide flight, he went searching. When he found the Land Rover in the car park with the keys still in it, he called the police.

From the start, it was a frustrating and delicate investigation. At first, as in most missing persons cases, police were sceptical. The odds were that the young wife of the wealthy, busy executive would turn up within hours or days, as 95 per cent of missing people do.

Next day, the ransom note turned up, and all bets that it was just an embarrassing domestic drama were off. This was life or death.

The note was typed, and postmarked in central Sydney. It demanded a $1 million ransom, which happened to be the exact amount of kidnap insurance Crown offers its executives and their families. This raised speculation that the kidnapper had inside information.

The note made conditions that baffled police. Contact would be made in ten days, through newspaper advertisements. And, it demanded that police not be told. Here, the kidnapper had miscalculated badly, because the note hadn't arrived until after the rattled husband raised the alarm.

Meanwhile, detectives combed through the Whelans' social and business contacts, looking for the classic suspect: someone with an opportunity and a motive. The common motives are greed, revenge or lust, sometimes all three.

Bruce Burrell's name came up quickly. Two reasons for this have been made public; if there are more links, the police weren't saying.

One reason is that Burrell telephoned Bernie Whelan out of the blue, the month before the abduction. If a coincidence, it was lousy timing. The other was the discovery that Burrell had visited the Whelans' place while Bernie Whelan was away, only days before the abduction. He had no good reason to go there.

There was no clue in Kerry Whelan's behaviour that anything was amiss in her life as a wealthy wife and devoted mother.

The days leading to her disappearance were filled with family engagements and meeting friends. Sunday 4 May was the 11th birthday of her youngest child, James. Her husband had arrived home the day before from one of his frequent overseas business trips.

On Monday, after dropping the children at school, Kerry went to a hairdresser and had a colour rinse put through her hair. That night the Whelans entertained neighbours.

Next morning she set off for Parramatta. On the way she dropped in on a friend, Marj Taylor, for coffee. She seemed normal and happy.

By 11 May, just five days after the abduction and more than a week before the story broke publicly, there were strange sights in the tiny hamlet of Bungonia, 200 kilometres and more than two hours' drive from Parramatta.

At first the tight-lipped strangers were coy about what they were doing, or as coy as you can be when hitting a township of a dozen houses in a fleet of shiny new cars with tinted glass and bristling with aerials, taking over two churches as temporary headquarters.

They could hardly deny being police, but they told curious locals that they were doing 'an exercise'. It didn't take people long to realise that they were watching Bruce Burrell's property, although no-one could have imagined why until after the kidnap became headlines on 21 May.

By then Bernie Whelan was begging for his wife's life. He was prepared to pay the ransom, but there were no takers.

In a videotaped appeal released on 23 May, the stricken man urged the 'kidnappers' to contact him, to let him know his wife was all right. 'For ten days we have tried to comply... with their ransom demands. For reasons unknown to us, the kidnappers have stopped contact. I would do whatever they asked, and I would go anywhere to get the safety of my wife.'

Detective Inspector Mick Howe, head of the kidnap taskforce, codenamed Operation Bellaire, said police supported Whelan and his company paying the ransom if it would ensure her safety.

There was no reply.

Asked on 25 May what had led police to Bungonia, Detective Sergeant Dennis Bray played the regulation straight bat, talking about following all leads and searching other properties. Asked if the man police were looking at had once worked for Crown, he intoned dutifully: 'I don't believe this has any consequence to this inquiry.'

But, in murder inquiries, the rule of thumb is that no confession and no body mostly means no case. After days of searching, surveillance and interviews had produced neither, police were not so keen to protect the identity or feelings of the man they rather quaintly termed 'a person of interest'. They pitched tents near his house, and for five days in late May combed the property, dragged dams and went through every inch of his home and sheds.

They found two suspected stolen cars, a Jaguar reportedly worth $150,000 and a Mitsubishi Pajero. Police also found weapons, including a .44 calibre Ruger semi-automatic rifle, stolen from Bernie Whelan, as well as a pistol and a prohibited crossbow.

It seemed that the jowly 44-year-old with glasses and a walrus moustache might look like a country bank manager, but he had some interesting hobbies. He became front-page news, the mystery man at the centre of the hunt for the millionaire's missing wife.

The publicity gave the task force what looked like its biggest break. That was when Sue Whitfield, a police officer at Maroubra, recognised Mr Burrell as someone local detectives had interviewed about the disappearance of Mrs Dorothy Davis almost exactly two years earlier. The odds seemed long against one man knowing two wealthy women who'd vanished.

The police turned the screw, sending dozens more searchers to comb hundreds of mineshafts and caves in rough country next to the Burrell farm. One reason was to try to find usable evidence. Another was to apply pressure.

More than three months after Kerry Whelan disappeared, little had changed. Except, perhaps, that Bruce Burrell voluntarily crossed the line that separates 'a person of interest' from a 'suspect' when he appeared on Channel Nine's tabloid current affairs show, *Sixty Minutes*. While it's likely Burrell had many thousands of good reasons to submit himself to the theatrical inquisition by Richard Carleton, it didn't look as if he was enjoying the chance to clear his name.

He confirmed that he had borrowed or 'minded' $100,000 for Dorothy Davis – but said he had paid her back in cash some time before her disappearance. There were, sadly, no witnesses to this transaction, which he admitted was 'bizarre'.

He said he was amazed about the chances of him knowing both Dorothy Davis and Kerry Whelan. 'It's freakish,' he said, shrugging. That's his story and he stuck to it – but it didn't save him.

In 1999 police charged Bruce Burrell with murdering Kerry Whelan. Charges were dropped but launched again after an inquest in 2002. He was sentenced to life for the Whelan murder in 2006 and convicted of Dorothy Davis's murder two years later. He died of lung and liver cancer in 2016, without revealing where he had hidden either body.

CHAPTER 11
STILL LOOKING FOR THE BEAUMONT CHILDREN

Who knew broken hearts could keep beating so long?

In 2019 Jim and Nancy Beaumont turned 93 and 91. For more than 50 years they'd woken every day to face the nightmare that their three children vanished from a crowded beach on Australia Day, 1966.

From the first days of their ordeal in that far-off summer, they feared the children were murdered – a probability that turned into a sickening certainty with every anniversary they've endured longer than most Australians have been alive.

There have been other abductions and murders, each as terrible as the next for the families left behind. But no other crime has grabbed the nation's imagination like the one still known simply as 'the Beaumont Children'. It is our version of the Lindbergh kidnapping in America, the Moors murders in Britain.

When a child vanishes, parents are condemned to the worst torment. But to lose all your children is beyond belief, loss on a scale that Australians imagine could only happen in wartime genocide far away.

The new year of 1966 was the start of a new era. Decimal currency was minted and printed ready for release on 14 February to replace pounds, shillings and pence; indestructible Prime Minister Robert Menzies was retiring after a phenomenal innings and rock 'n' roll was taking over popular culture as the baby boom turned into a tidal wave of teenagers dancing to a brand new beat.

Times were changing – but some things hadn't, which meant an anonymous monster could move among us without trace.

It's hard for anyone born since the 1960s to imagine a world with no credit cards, no computers, no security cameras, no mobile telephones and only primitive recording equipment: none of the things, in fact, that now make it almost impossible for anyone to move around without leaving an electronic trail.

One technological advance actually made life easier for wrongdoers: cars, scarce in the 1950s, were by 1966 relatively plentiful and affordable, so that anyone who had one could move across a city, a state or the entire country almost as easily as we can today – but without being automatically recorded along the way.

Whoever lured Jane, Arnna and Grant Beaumont from

Glenelg Beach that hot afternoon faced nothing more than the uncertain impressions of random eyewitnesses.

Satellites circled the planet and scientists were close to putting man on the moon, but forensic science and security surveillance techniques lagged well behind the space race: in 1966, the odds still were that an unknown offender not actually caught at a crime scene could get away with murder, probably in a car with bodies in the boot.

In the Beaumont case, he has got away with it for half a century. It was probably the crime that did most to change Australians' perception of safety. We went from a casual and carefree society in which most kids played unsupervised to a grave new world in which parents live in fear children will be harmed.

It was the end of innocence. So who was the killer that changed a nation?

Inevitably, the 50th anniversary of the Beaumont case in the summer of early 2016 prompted what is called a 'new lead'. Odds are it was just the latest of the many 'tips' given to police over the years, and almost certainly just another cross-out on a list of dead ends.

Such 'leads' have come from the mentally ill, from cruel hoaxers and from sincere well-meaning people. They all share one thing: so far, not one has been useful. Neither has the police work that began with a bizarre artist's impression of the thin, blond man with the Beaumont children when last seen.

It was, after all, Australia Day, and the artist (and, no doubt, many police and reporters) had been celebrating in traditional style – beer, burned sausages and more beer – before being called in that evening.

The artist would later admit he was so liquored up he could hardly hold his pen, which explains why the sketch looks more like an alien than human. It was a bad start to an investigation that never got much better.

From the beginning, the case attracted stunts that made headlines but no headway in the investigation. The first was the arrival of celebrity corrupt cop Ray 'Gunner' Kelly, flown from Sydney by a newspaper not to make an arrest so much as to create a sensation.

Kelly, the Roger Rogerson of the time, left town after just one day, his mission accomplished: he had posed for photographs, tossed off a few quotable lines and no doubt pocketed his fee. It was a circus. So was the arrival a few months later of a Dutch 'clairvoyant', Gerard Croiset, who led investigators and reporters around randomly before predicting the children's bodies would be found under or near a new building that had been under construction at the time.

A public subscription paid for concrete to be dug up. Nothing was found. Decades later, when the building was demolished, the entire site was dug over, but still nothing.

The police, meanwhile, plodded on, fielding letters and calls and checking 'sightings' of the children all over Australia and beyond. Each lead gave the tortured parents hope, only to dash it again and again. For years Nancy Beaumont insisted on staying at their now haunted house, in case her kids came home.

Probably no one except the killer – if he's still alive – knows who did it. The odds against the case being solved before Jim and Nancy Beaumont die are 1000-1 and drifting. The killer is either an 'unknown unknown' – a secret psychopath who has never come to police attention – or a 'known unknown', one of a few viable suspects linked to the crime by flimsy circumstantial evidence and hearsay.

Only one of that group is still alive, and he is in his 70s. He is Bevan Spencer von Einem, and authorities will keep finding reasons to keep him in jail.

Von Einem was an accountant by profession, a depraved sex killer by compulsion. He was arrested and later convicted over the abduction, torture and murder of Richard Kelvin, teenage son of Adelaide TV news reader Rob Kelvin.

Young Kelvin's abused body was found in bushland outside Adelaide six weeks after he vanished near his parents' home on 5 June, 1983. Experts believe he had been kept alive most of that time, in a drugged state, eventually dying from internal injuries inflicted with a bottle or other blunt object.

It is unlikely von Einem acted alone. It is known he bribed transvestites with drugs to lure young men into cars, and that he knew a core group of at least three other deviates.

Some police believe the group, dubbed 'The Family', included a businessman, a doctor, a lawyer and the brother of an Olympic athlete. They have been able to avoid arrest while von Einem serves his sentence and keeps silent about who else participated in the murders of Kelvin and four other young men abducted between 1979 and 1983.

In 1966 von Einem was turning 21. It would later be revealed he was spotted in film taken at Glenelg beach days after the Beaumont children disappeared. Deviant offenders are drawn to the scenes of their crimes.

Some think von Einem's relative youthfulness in 1966 makes it unlikely he was the killer. It is not a persuasive argument, as the sexual sadism he demonstrated in the Kelvin case would have surfaced at puberty.

Another argument against von Einem as a suspect is

that witnesses estimated that the thin, blond man they saw with the children was probably 'in his 30s'. Witnesses are notoriously unreliable in describing anything seen fleetingly, and police sometimes confuse or distort what a witness means, so it is risky to discount suspects as 'too young' or 'too old' on the basis of statements that can no longer be checked.

As for von Einem being capable of a triple murder at his age, at least one other suspect demonstrated he was a compulsive sexual psychopath when barely in his teens. Even as a child, Derek Edward Percy did things that meant his mother never left him alone with other children.

While at school at Mt Beauty, where his father was an engineer, he would steal and wear women's underclothes and display violent sexual fetishes.

Percy, who died in 2013, has become a prime suspect for the Wanda Beach murders, which happened in Sydney a year before the Beaumont children vanished.

At Wanda Beach, a teenager matching the then 17-year-old Percy's description was seen near 15-year-olds Christine Sharrock and Marianne Schmidt not long before they were killed together. Alcohol was found in their systems, which tallies with 'plans' Percy wrote, found after he was arrested more than four years later for murdering 12-year-old Yvonne Tuohy at Warneet in Victoria.

At the time of the Wanda Beach murders, he lived just two kilometres from where both girls lived. When Percy killed Yvonne Tuohy he was a naval cadet at the nearby HMAS Cerberus training base.

Police who worked on the Tuohy murder had no doubt Percy would have been capable of similar crimes in his early teens. Other cases were linked to him by 'similar fact' and circumstantial evidence.

He became the main suspect not just for the Wanda Beach horror but for the murder of Simon Brook, 3, killed in Sydney in 1968, and for the murder of Allen Redston, 6, in Canberra in 1966. And he would eventually be named by a coroner as the murderer of Linda Stilwell at St Kilda in 1968.

There was a common denominator: most of the murders were near water and Percy had been in the vicinity at the time.

Percy's father had introduced him to sailing relatively young – perhaps as a way to occupy an obviously disturbed boy.

Father and son had a small yacht, which they towed to regattas, often interstate. One of the most popular regattas on the sailing calendar was held off Glenelg on the Australia Day weekend in 1966. Percy was barely 18 then but if he'd killed two 15-year-old girls at Wanda Beach a year earlier, there was nothing to stop him killing nine-year-old Jane, seven-year-old Arnna and Grant, 4.

Against the theory is that the Beaumonts' bodies were never found, suggesting cool planning and local knowledge rather than an impulsive crime by a teenage visitor. Then again, even evil people can get lucky. Percy was lucky his respectable parents apparently never suspected anything sinister about their strange son. Because where he went, children were killed.

The same could be said for a far more sophisticated child killer. By the time he was jailed for murdering a little boy in Tasmania in 1975, the smooth-talking murderer who called himself James Ryan O'Neill was 27. The Scotch College old boy from Melbourne had been raised as Leigh Anthony Bridgart.

He had fled Melbourne for outback Western Australia in 1971 after being charged with 12 counts of abducting and molesting children. While he was in the Kimberley a young Aboriginal boy, Jimmy Patrick Taylor, went missing, presumed murdered. Two months later O'Neill moved as far as he could – to Tasmania.

In 1975, O'Neill was heading to pick up his wife and newborn son from hospital when he abducted and killed a nine-year-old boy, Ricky John Smith. Before police caught him, he murdered another young boy, Bruce Colin Wilson.

He was arrested trying to abduct two more boys.

Retired Victorian detective Gordon Davie and a former crime reporter, Janine Widgery, interviewed O'Neill in prison. He said he'd committed his first murder at 15, in 1962. And he mentioned the Beaumonts.

Davie was intrigued that O'Neill did not deny murdering the Beaumonts, instead evasively saying he lived in Melbourne at the time, not Adelaide. But Davie found that O'Neill had visited the Coober Pedy opal fields – via Adelaide – about 15 times. Something he said convinced Davie he had disposed of a body – or bodies – in one of the thousands of abandoned mine shafts there.

Davie puts O'Neill on a 'very short list' of suspects for the Beaumont case. He says a sex killer doesn't start offending at 27, O'Neill's age when he was finally arrested. He had roamed Australia for a decade before that. And everywhere he went, children went missing.

Arthur Stanley Brown was an old man when he was named prime suspect for killing two little sisters in August 1970 in his home town of Townsville. Susan Mackay was five, Judith was seven. They vanished as they walked to school. Their bodies were found in scrub outside town two days later.

Brown was so well-known in Townsville he was invisible. As a government maintenance worker, he worked on police stations, courthouses and schools and enjoyed the perk of five weeks' annual leave, which allowed him to travel interstate.

Local teachers, police and lawyers all knew the neat, lean little man well enough not to give him a second thought. But they didn't know him as well as younger members of his wife's extended family.

They knew he was a child molester but kept their sordid secret until one woman finally spoke out, suspecting something even more sinister.

That was in 1998, when Arthur Brown was 86, although still plainly recognisable as the lantern-jawed character photographed soon after World War II. He'd looked fit, and much younger than his years, for decades.

With his wide-brimmed hat on, he could pass for someone many years younger.

Brown's first wife died in suspicious circumstances in 1978. His second wife was the dead woman's younger sister, a tiny woman who pandered to his tastes by wearing children's pyjamas to bed.

When the police finally came for him, Brown didn't seem shocked. But he blurted something about the Mackay sisters' murders that a prosecutor would later label 'consciousness of guilt.'

As soon as he got a lawyer, Brown fell silent, and developed symptoms of dementia that would ultimately see murder charges dropped on grounds that he wasn't fit to plead.

One problem in prosecuting him was that all his work records had been lost – including, crucially, when he had taken leave.

Which was a pity, because it might have indicated if he was on one of his regular interstate motoring holidays in 1973, when Joanne Ratcliffe and Kirste Gordon went missing in Adelaide.

Several witnesses saw a thin-faced man wearing a wide-brimmed hat carrying a small girl and leading a bigger one from Adelaide Oval that day. When police compared identikit sketches of that suspect with photographs of Arthur Brown, the resemblance was striking.

Whether the same thin-faced man had been at the city's Glenelg Beach on Australia Day seven years earlier, in 1966, no one knows.

Officially, the case has never closed, but time is against it.

Chances are, only one person can help. Somewhere out there is a man who was tall and thin and blond in 1966. Somewhere, in a dusty family album, there might be a snapshot of him in navy blue bathers. Someone, somewhere, must suspect who he is.

Jim and Nancy Beaumont have lived apart for many years but are united in grief that only their own deaths will end. They lost their children then they lost each other. Now, as they face the tenth decade of their shattered lives, they are starting to outlive their contemporaries.

Almost as if they're hanging on, waiting for the kids to find their way home.

Nancy Beaumont died in September 2019, aged 92. Jim Beaumont died in April 2023. He was 97.

ABOUT THE AUTHOR

Andrew Rule joined his first newspaper exactly two years before the Easey Street murders. Since then, he has covered everything from the Olympic Games and horse racing to natural disasters and trouble spots around the world but, in Australia, he has written mostly about crime in Melbourne newspapers, national magazines and books. The Easey Street case has always resonated with him because his mother's family were friends with Suzanne Armstrong's parents and grandparents at Strathbogie in the 1940s. He met the Armstrongs when they visited his family in Gippsland in the 1960s.